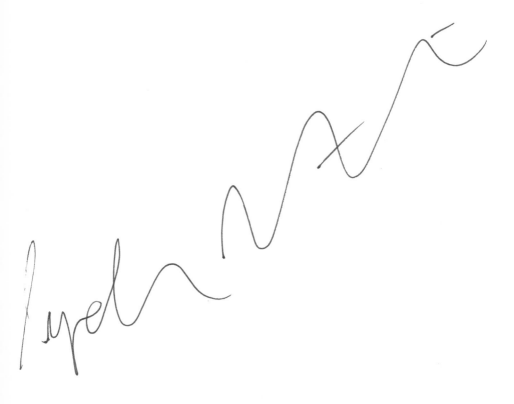

Think Again

Think Again

Why Good Leaders Make
Bad Decisions and How to Keep It
From Happening to You

Sydney Finkelstein, Jo Whitehead,
and Andrew Campbell

Harvard Business Press
Boston, Massachusetts

Library of Congress Cataloging-in-Publication Data
Finkelstein, Sydney.
    Think again : why good leaders make bad decisions and how to keep it from happening
to you / Sydney Finkelstein, Jo Whitehead and Andrew Campbell.
        p.   cm.
    ISBN 978-1-4221-2612-7 (hardcover: alk. paper)
    1. Decision making. 2. Leadership. I. Whitehead, Jo. II. Campbell, Andrew, 1950
Aug. 3- III. Title.
HD30.23.F555 2009
658.4'092—dc22

                                                                      2008043317

CONTENTS

ACKNOWLEDGMENTS

This book relied on the contribution and support of many individuals—many of whom would understandably prefer not to be mentioned by name.

Those whom we can mention include our colleagues at the Ashridge Strategic Management Centre (ASMC)—including Marcus Alexander, Felix Barber, Stephen Bungay, Anthony Freeling, and Mike Goold—who provided regular comments and input to the many drafts of our material. The member companies of ASMC also provided guidance and inspiration. Particular individuals from those companies whom we would like to mention include Peter van Laarhoven and Phil Renshaw. We benefited from the editing support of John Butman, Stuart Crainer, and Des Dearlove, as well as our editor at Harvard Business Press, Jeff Kehoe. Other input, examples, and advice came from Martin Essayan, Nick Viner, Valentin Von Massow, Liz McMeikan, Simon Wilsher, Peter Bennell, Simon Farnborough, Penny Dash, Cam Middleton, Dima Podpolny, Neil Monnery, Judi Bevan, Ulrich Pidun, Bob Batt, and Jay Kim.

Jo Whitehead would especially like to thank his PhD supervisors, John Stopford and John Hunt—who started him down the road of researching decision making. He dedicates this book to Monica, whose decision to marry him he trusts was not hopelessly flawed.

Sydney Finkelstein would like to acknowledge the generous support of the Tuck School at Dartmouth College, and especially Deans Paul Danos and Bob Hansen for their continuing confidence that there is so much to learn from studying what goes wrong, and why. Thanks also go to the MBA students and executives who road tested some of the ideas in the book, especially the Hurricane Katrina story. The steady efforts of Helen Reese, agent extraordinaire, are greatly appreciated, as always. He dedicates this book to his daughter Erica, who has already made many well-considered decisions and has many more to come.

Andrew Campbell would especially like to thank his coauthors, Jo and Sydney, for tolerating his robust challenges, frequent edits, and continuous pressure for completion. Without their willingness to have another go, take the time required, and reject some of his suggestions, the ideas in this book would not be so powerful.

—Sydney Finkelstein, Jo Whitehead,
   and Andrew Campbell
   Hanover, New Hampshire, and London
   October 2008

Decision making lies at the heart of our personal and professional lives. Every day we make decisions. Some are small, domestic, and innocuous. Others are more important—decisions that affect people's lives, livelihoods, and well-being. Inevitably, we make mistakes along the way. We are only human—even when we are at work. Indeed, the daunting reality is that enormously important decisions made by intelligent, responsible people with the best information and intentions sometimes go wrong.

Good leaders make bad decisions. Even great leaders can make bad decisions.

President Kennedy is famous for his blunder over the Bay of Pigs. President Hoover failed to inflate the economy after the great crash of 1929. Margaret Thatcher, the British prime minister, championed a "poll tax" that contributed to her being ousted by her own party. Paul Wolfowitz, the former U.S. deputy secretary of defense, was asked to resign as president of the World Bank because of a pay settlement related to his partner, who also worked at the bank.

And it's not just politicians and public servants who get it badly wrong; business leaders, too, are prone to misjudgment. Juergen Schrempp, CEO of Daimler-Benz, led the merger of Chrysler and Daimler-Benz against internal opposition. Nearly ten years later, Daimler was forced to virtually give Chrysler away in a private equity deal. Lee Kun Hee, CEO of Samsung, pushed his company into a disastrous investment in automobiles. As losses mounted, he was forced to sell the car division for a tenth of the billions he had invested. An Wang, founder of the electronics company Wang, insisted on a proprietary operating system for his company's personal computer, even after it was clear that the IBM PC would become the industry standard. The company is now history.

Whether the decision is a personal one, as in the case of Wolfowitz, or of global importance, as in the case of the U.S. government reaction to the financial crisis in the late 1920s, mistakes happen. But why do good leaders make bad decisions? And how can we reduce the risk of its happening to us?

The Decisive Heart

To find out, we traveled to the heart of decision making in organizations of all shapes and sizes throughout the world. Each of the authors brought his particular perspective to the problem. As one of the world's leading researchers into corporate strategy, for example, Andrew has been privy to some of the most important decisions made in some of the world's biggest companies. While, in his research—captured in his bestselling book, *Why Smart Executives Fail*—Sydney has examined the intricacies of failure. Finally, from his doctoral research on decision making and his years with The Boston Consulting Group, Jo has a unique combination of intellectual rigor and practical experience. What linked all our work and brought us together was a fascination with not just why bad decisions are made, but also what can be done to mitigate the dangers.

This unique combination of backgrounds and perspectives has been supplemented by our joint research. We began by assembling a database of decisions that went wrong. Let's be clear: we were not looking for decisions that simply turned out badly. We were looking for decisions that were flawed at the time they were made. This is an important point. It isn't that with twenty-twenty hindsight we identified these decisions as flawed. We sought out decisions in which any clearheaded analysis at the time would have concluded that it was the wrong decision.

Of course, many bad outcomes are due to bad luck or to taking calculated risks. In the business and political worlds in particular, sensible decisions based on considered thinking can turn out badly thanks to the unavoidable risks involved. Sometimes people are just unlucky.

As you can imagine, trying to distinguish between flawed decisions and calculated risks that turned out badly is not easy. For each, we made an assessment. Given the information available at the time, did we think that a reasonably competent person would have made the same decision?

We also looked for dissenting views in the decision-making process. The existence of contrary views is not proof that a decision is wrong. Many decisions have contrary views. But if there were no contrary views at the time, we excluded the decision from our rapidly expanding collection.

We quickly found there are an awful lot of bad decisions out there! Indeed, in unfamiliar circumstances, such as businesses entering new markets or politicians coping with new challenges, flawed decisions abound. We did not find it hard to identify eighty-three of them (appendix I lists the entire database of decisions we studied).

We are not claiming that we have a unique ability to spot flawed decisions. Indeed, some of the decisions we examine may be considered by others as wise choices that turned out badly. Fortunately, our argument does not depend on whether our examples are correctly categorized. Our understanding of why flawed decisions are so common comes from the work that has been done by neuroscientists and decision scientists to understand how the brain works when faced with a set of circumstances that require a decision.

Flaws of the Jungle

So what did we find in our quest to understand why capable people make errors of judgment? The answers were simpler and more powerful than we were expecting.

Two factors are at play in a flawed decision: an individual or a group of individuals who have made an error of judgment, and a decision process that fails to correct the error. Both have to be present to produce a bad decision. This was an important realization. A bad decision starts with at least one influential person making an error of judgment. But normally, the decision process will save the day: facts will be brought to the table that challenge the flawed thinking, or other people with different views will influence the outcome. So the second factor that contributes to a bad decision is the way the decision is managed: for whatever reason, as the decision is being discussed, the erroneous views are not exposed and corrected.

As a result, we began to focus our research on how our brains make decisions. Part 1 describes how the brain has been wonderfully de-signed for decision making—but also how it can be tricked into false judgments.

Part 2 describes the four conditions under which flawed thinking is most likely to happen. We call these *red flag conditions* because they provide a warning that when these conditions exist, even an experi-enced decision maker may get it wrong. Complex decisions, involving interpretation and judgment, are difficult to get right. You need de-bate—but how do you know when you or the other party is arguing from a biased position? You need consensus—but how do you know when your consensus is really groupthink? What is needed is a diagnostic for knowing when the risk of being wrong is at its highest—when the deci-sion makers need to step back and "think again." Our red flag condi-tions are a simple, but not simplistic tool to help decision makers know when to pause for breath—when you need to take special steps to make sure that a decision does not go off the rails.

Part 3 describes what you can do about it. Unlike other writers in this increasingly popular field we believe that it is impractical for us to correct our own mental processes. The brain's way of working makes this solution particularly difficult. Hence, when there are red flag condi-tions, we recommend *safeguards* that are external to the individual. We describe four types of safeguard; each helps to strengthen the deci-sion process, so that the influence of distorted thinking is diluted or challenged.

Safeguards reduce the risk that red flag conditions will lead to a bad decision: they act as a counterweight (see figure I-1). Choosing safeguards is not mechanical. There is no direct link between a particular red flag condition and a particular safeguard. Instead, safeguards need to be chosen not only with an understanding of the red flag conditions but also with knowledge of the people and the organization, as well as a healthy skepticism of too much bureaucracy.

Our red flags and safeguards framework not only helps defend against bad decisions, it also helps cut back on bureaucracy. In many organizations, governance processes and decision rules have been developed with the intention of defending the organization against all possible errors in decision making. Each major blunder leads to additional processes and rules that are applied to all major decisions. The result is a bureaucracy that is costly, time consuming, and demotivating. Most importantly, managers start to lose respect for the system and seek ways of circumventing the processes.

Armed with our red flags and safeguards framework, leaders can now strip away much of this standardized bureaucracy. For decisions where there are no red flags, the decision process can be fast and simple. But for decisions with red flags, leaders can design appropriate safeguards

FIGURE I-1

Safeguards can defend against the risk of error

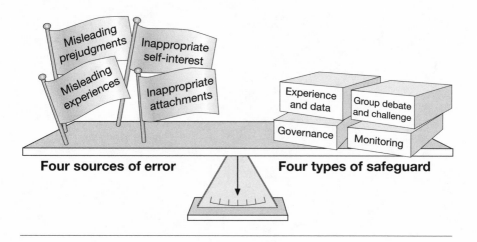

that are more likely to be effective and less likely to demotivate or dehumanize the managers involved. In other words, we are not recommending *more* process but *more targeted* process. In chapter 10 we give guidance on how to do this.

Of course, it is not possible to eliminate all the risks. Even armed with our safeguards framework, leaders will still make mistakes—but it is possible to improve the odds. Further advice and ideas can be found on our Web site, www.thinkagain-book.com. Our hope is that *Think Again* will help decision makers talk about an issue that everyone recognizes but does not have a way of discussing. If we have one ambition for the book, it is to legitimize more discussion about red flag conditions and to energize people everywhere to feel comfortable raising issues of decision process design. The simple questions "Are there any red flags here?" and "Have we got a good process for this decision?" should be as common as "What decision are we trying to make?" or "Who is making this decision?"

It won't guarantee you never make a bad decision again—what book could?—but it will enable you to better understand why decisions go wrong, and help protect yourself and your colleagues from the inevitable errors of judgment you will make.

PART ONE

How Your Brain Makes Decisions

ONE

In the Eye of the Storm

A S HURRICANE KATRINA increased in intensity in August 2005, the Federal Emergency Management Agency (FEMA) started preparing. "New Orleans is of particular concern because much of that city lies below sea level. If hurricane winds blow from a certain direction, there are dire predictions of what may happen in the city," it reported on Saturday, August 27.[1] The report was distributed to top officials at the Department of Homeland Security (DHS). One of the recipients was Matthew Broderick.

As the director of the Homeland Security Operations Center in Washington, D.C., Matthew Broderick was in charge of the clearinghouse for information on domestic events of potential significance, such as terrorist activities, border crossings, and natural disasters. The operations center collected information from public service organizations across the country. By the time FEMA issued its warning, there were serious concerns that Katrina might hit New Orleans, a scenario that the Department of Homeland Security had identified in 2003 as one of the nation's top fifteen potential disasters, natural or otherwise. (Scenario 1 was the detonation of a ten-kiloton nuclear device in Washington, D.C.)

Matthew Broderick was in the hot seat. When asked, during a subsequent Senate committee hearing, who was responsible for informing

Secretary Michael Chertoff, head of Homeland Security, and President George Bush of the state of affairs in New Orleans, Broderick replied, "It was my responsibility. If they did not receive reports of the flooding, it was my fault."[2] It was also Broderick's responsibility to alert Secretary Chertoff of the need to "stand up" the Interagency Incident Management Group (IIMG), a mechanism for coordinating a proactive federal response to disasters.

Hurricane Katrina hit the southern coast of America on the Monday morning, August 29, near Buras, Louisiana, 55 miles south of New Orleans. Although it was not the doomsday Category 5 hurricane feared, it was a fiercer-than-average Category 3 storm with 125-mile-per-hour winds. As the full fury of Katrina was unleashed, it deposited between six and twelve inches of rain on the area and sent a twelve-foot storm surge into Lake Pontchartrain, devastating the lakefront area and smashing yachts and buildings into pulp. St. Bernard and Plaquemines parishes to the east and south of the city were overwhelmed, and the city's electrical grid was wiped out. Communication networks were destroyed, roads were flooded, bridges collapsed, and fires burned out of control. Even the city's famous sports arena—the Superdome, eventually home to some 25,000 refugees—was mauled by the storm and left without power. The much-feared "New Orleans" scenario was unfolding. And yet, Matthew Broderick went home that evening believing that reports of a disaster in New Orleans were exaggerated.

So how did this seemingly extraordinary error of judgment occur? Why did Broderick delay so long? To make sense of Matthew Broderick's inaction, we have to understand how events unfolded and the factors that affected Broderick's thinking—including how his own background and previous experiences colored the way his brain processed the information he received.

Data Points

Broderick set up the operations center in 2003. He had three hundred staff members; representatives from forty-five federal, state, and local agencies; and a budget of $40 million. He was well suited to the job, with thirty years' experience running operations centers for the Marine Corps, including such tasks as the evacuations from Saigon and Phnom Penh.[3]

The first reports of major flooding and possible damage to levees began arriving in the operations center at 8:30 a.m. on Monday the twenty-ninth, some two and a half hours after Katrina had hit the coast. Broderick's experience told him that first reports are often inaccurate or exaggerated. So he spent the rest of Monday trying to get confirmed information from reliable sources.

By 5:00 p.m., the operations center had received at least nine reports of levee breaches and eight other reports of major flooding. But there was also conflicting information. The Army Corps of Engineers was consistently reporting that there were no levee breaches, and FEMA, the agency on the ground, claimed that it was coping. By 6:00 p.m., Broderick needed to put out a situation report to Secretary Chertoff and the White House. Reflecting afterward Broderick mentioned two sources of information that influenced his report: the Army Corps of Engineers, and a CNN report:

The Corps of Engineers kept telling us that, no, nothing had broken. Nothing had been breached, but there was some water that was going into the city. But flooding takes place in every hurricane—Dade County, the Keys, and all of that. So as long as the levees weren't breaking, we felt that they were still safe.[4]

The only one data point that I really had, personally, visually [on TV], was the celebration in the streets of New Orleans of people drinking beer and partying because—and they used— they came up with the word, "We dodged the bullet." And they were celebrating in New Orleans. So I'm looking at partying Monday night in the City of New Orleans, celebrating in the French Quarter that they had "dodged a bullet." So that's a pretty good indicator right there, regardless of what information I'm getting, that things looked relatively calm. There's always flooding after a hurricane. We experience that in Florida all the time. There's always power outages. But the

*catastrophic fear of levees crashing in and people drowning
and blowing people away appeared not to have happened, and
there was a sigh of relief.[5]*

Situation report 7 issued at 6:00 p.m. stated, "Preliminary reports indicate the levees in New Orleans have not been breached; however, an
assessment is still pending."[6] Broderick then headed home, content
that the bullet had been dodged.

As Broderick slept, information continued to stream into the operations center. Some of the most detailed information came from a FEMA
public relations officer who had been on a Coast Guard helicopter Monday afternoon for a visual survey of the city. He reported a quarter-mile
breach in one levee and that more than two-thirds of the city was under
water.[7] The head of FEMA was on CNN with Larry King on Monday
night and described the situation in New Orleans as "a catastrophic disaster."[8] With this information in hand, the night shift at Broderick's operations center published situation report 8 at 6:00 a.m. Tuesday
morning, declaring that multiple levees had been breached and that
much of downtown New Orleans was under water.

Back in his office on Tuesday morning, Broderick read situation report 8. He was not inclined to believe it. At 8:13 a.m. he sent an e-mail
to the White House and several top DHS staffers, suggesting that report
8 might be an exaggeration. He stated that the levee breaches were
"being assessed," and that "there is no major damages but MAY require
significant air asset to lift the stranded personnel."[9]

"Tuesday is when we were really pushing. Are these breaches, or are
these overtoppings? Where are they? What's the extent? What's being
flooded? I mean, it could have been flooding a swamp, as far as we
knew," Broderick later explained.[10] He finally got the truth he was looking for late Tuesday morning. Colonel Richard Wagenaar, the commander of the New Orleans district Army Corps of Engineers, had tried
to check the status of the levees on Monday but was unable to get
around the city by car. Tuesday morning he found a helicopter to take
him on his first survey of the levee system. The colonel counted four

breaches in the Industrial Canal levee and a massive breach in the 17th Street Canal.

Broderick then alerted Secretary Chertoff that the levees had indeed been breached, and he recommended standing up the Interagency Incident Management Group. Two hours later, the White House received confirmation that the levees had been breached. Thirty hours after Hurricane Katrina made landfall in Louisiana, the IIMG was activated, and the Department of Homeland Security decided that Katrina was a larger-than-average disaster.[11]

On Monday night, Matthew Broderick went home having decided that New Orleans had dodged the bullet. Moreover, he did not believe report 8 when he read it the next morning. His decisions on Monday and early Tuesday delayed the federal response by some twenty-four hours, causing greater suffering for the people of New Orleans, contributing to a perception that the DHS and the federal government were incompetent, and resulting, ultimately, in a loss of face for the United States on the global stage.

Katrina caused catastrophic damage. Hundreds of thousands of people lost their homes—many permanently. At least 1,800 people died. The total cost of the damage was estimated at $86 billion. And yet, many hours were lost as Broderick gathered information and then made the wrong decision.

Brains at Work

Matthew Broderick is not the first manifestly competent leader to make an error of judgment, and he will not be the last. Let's be clear: he was extremely well qualified for his job. He had lots of relevant experience and an array of information at his fingertips. His integrity and ability are not in doubt. But he got it wrong—very wrong. Throughout Monday, a nightmare had been unfolding in New Orleans. So why didn't Broderick act sooner?

Errors of judgment—big and small—start in the heads of individuals, people like Matthew Broderick. So we needed to understand how the brain works. Of course, there are plenty of books and articles about how people *ought* to make decisions. Most of them suggest something along the following lines:

- Lay out the problem.

- Define the objectives.

- Generate options.

- Evaluate each option against the objectives and other relevant criteria.

- Choose the option with the best outcome.

- Monitor progress and change course if necessary.

But we weren't really interested in how the books say people should make decisions, or even what decision makers say about how they reach their judgments. We wanted to understand what goes on inside the brain when people make decisions. We wanted to understand what was going on inside Matthew Broderick's head when he got it wrong.

What we found was that our brains use two processes that enable us to cope with the complexities we face: *pattern recognition* and *emotional tagging*. Both help us make excellent decisions most of the time, which is why they have been selected as we have evolved. But in certain conditions they can mislead us.

Pattern recognition helps us assess inputs we receive. It is not like flicking through a book of photographs in order to identify someone. We do not simply search our memories for an exact image match. It is much more complex. Even a simple task such as visual recognition involves thirty different parts of the brain. Each part of the brain focuses on a different type of input and looks for a memory of past inputs that matches it. An integrating function then takes the signals about what matches have been found, makes assumptions about missing bits of information, and arrives at a point of view.[12] We say more about pattern recognition in chapter 2.

Most of the time, pattern recognition works remarkably well. But there are important exceptions. If we are faced with unfamiliar inputs—especially if the unfamiliar inputs appear familiar—we can think we recognize something when we do not. We refer to this as the problem of *misleading experiences*. Our brains may contain memories of past experiences that connect with inputs we are receiving. Unfortunately, the past experiences are not a good match with the current situation and hence mislead us.

Another exception is when our thinking has been primed before we receive the inputs, by, for example, previous judgments or decisions we have made that connect with the current situation. If these judgments are inappropriate for the current situation, they disrupt our pattern recognition processes, causing us to misjudge the information we are receiving. We refer to these as *misleading prejudgments*.

In other words, our pattern recognition process is fallible. We have all experienced the embarrassment of accosting a complete stranger we thought we recognized. We have also experienced some degree of terror because we have misjudged the sharpness of a bend in the road or the speed of an oncoming car. What is less obvious is that our pattern recognition processes can also let us down when we are trying to judge the severity of a financial crisis, the value of an acquisition target, or the threat from an incoming hurricane.

The second process that helps us cope with complexity is emotional tagging. Emotions are essential for decision making. This may be a surprise to those of you who pride yourselves on your ability to be analytical and rational. But the evidence from decision scientists and neuroscientists is clear: we find it difficult to focus our thinking without emotional input.

Emotions are part of decision making because we tag our thoughts and memories with emotions. These tags, when triggered by a pattern recognition match, tell us whether to pay attention to something or ignore it, and they give us an action orientation. For example, our brain will process a noise from the street outside and decide to ignore it because it has no significant emotional tag. But if the noise is a frightened cry from a child, our brain will make us immediately alert, and it will suggest a plan of action—go to the window and check what is happening—before we are even aware that we need to do something. This is because these sounds are associated with strong emotional tags such as fear and love. We explore emotional tagging more fully in chapter 3.

Our emotional tags enable us to act with speed, guiding us to be alert to the critical inputs and to select a plan of action instantaneously. However, in some circumstances, our emotional tags can get in the way of good decision making. In particular, when we have emotional tags that are inappropriate for the decision we are making, our thinking can be distorted. For example, when we are faced with a business decision about whether to cut costs or not, the emotional loyalty we feel toward existing staff can cause us to favor the status quo even when we are trying to be objective and evenhanded. The emotional tag makes the status quo option—no cuts—seem more attractive to us even though we may not be fully aware of why.

Emotional tags can be a problem for us in four ways. The first two are about misleading experiences and misleading prejudgments: emotions attached to these experiences or prejudgments can give them more prominence in our thinking than is appropriate. The result is often an inappropriate action orientation. Think about the impact of vertigo or of a fear of dogs. We may know rationally that there is no danger, but we can be unable to control our thoughts or actions. The third and fourth ways emotional tags can disrupt our thinking are through *inappropriate attachments*, such as the attachment we might feel to colleagues when considering whether to cut costs, and the much more familiar *inappropriate self-interest*, which lies behind the attention the press gives to the personal interests of politicians or the attention managers give to aligning incentives.

So our journey into the brain identified four conditions that can disrupt our thinking and lead us to believe that our point of view is sound when it is not. We think of these as red flag conditions—as when a red flag is put on a beach to warn bathers of dangerous weather conditions. Misleading experiences, misleading prejudgments, inappropriate self-interest, and inappropriate attachments are four root causes of errors in thinking that lead to bad decisions.

Decisively Unconscious

The errors in our thinking that can happen when pattern recognition or emotional tagging misleads us would not be such a problem if we made decisions in a controlled, easy-to-audit way that involved plenty of checks and balances. Unfortunately, we do not. Much of our mental processing is unconscious, which makes it hard to check. We will say more about unconscious thinking throughout part 1.

In addition to high levels of unconscious thinking, we also make decisions using limited checks and feedback loops. We have labeled this the *one-plan-at-a-time process*: most of the time, we assess the situation; we think of a plan of action; we then imagine how this plan will work out; and we only consider another plan if we spot some problem with the first plan we thought of.

If we have misjudged the situation because of faulty pattern recognition or inappropriate emotional tags, the one-plan-at-a-time process only gives us limited chances of correcting our errors. For example, when we hear the cry of a frightened child, it might be better to rush downstairs into the street rather than waste time by going to the window to see what is happening. We do not normally juggle these two alternatives in our mind before acting, because the first plan, going to the window to see what is happening, seems so sensible. Once our pattern recognition and emotional tags suggest an action, we normally go for it if the imagined outcome seems reasonable based on our experience. Chapter 4 is devoted to the one-plan-at-a-time process.

This explanation of what goes on in the brain may seem rather simplistic—Neanderthal, even—and far removed from high-powered decision making that occurs in business or government. We have not referred to the influence of other people, for instance, or the requirement in many decision processes to carry out in-depth analysis of the situation, to lay out the options, or to involve those concerned in the decision. These will be addressed in part 3. Remember, in part 1 we are trying to understand what goes on inside the brain of an individual when he or she is faced with a decision. The core message from this journey through the brain is that our thinking processes are prone to error in certain types of situations and only have limited capability to correct the errors once we have made them.

The Brain and Matthew Broderick

Let's consider Matthew Broderick's thinking. What might have gone through his mind on that fateful Monday?

The process began when Broderick received inputs about Katrina. He would have registered Katrina as a threat to New Orleans, but his pattern recognition processes must have seen Katrina as a familiar threat. He had experienced many hurricanes before. As a result, his emotional tags did not suggest any need for unusual actions. He did not appear to ask for extra information about New Orleans or the nature of the risk. Nor did he put in place special mechanisms that would help him make the difficult judgments he subsequently had to make. To understand his reaction—or rather his lack of reaction—it is important to remember that he had previously experienced lots of hurricane warnings, none of which had required the operations center to alert the federal support mechanisms, at least until the damage could be properly assessed. As it turned out, these proved to be misleading experiences.

On Monday the twenty-ninth, Broderick began to receive inputs about flooding in New Orleans. From previous crisis work, he had learned not to overreact to early reports. He had learned to give them a neutral emotional tag. He had also learned to look for a particular type of information, something that Broderick referred to afterward as "ground truth." This was a prejudgment he had made, and it proved to be a misleading prejudgment. Given the special situation in New Orleans, where much of the land is below sea level, waiting for ground truth could result in tragic delays.

Consistent with the one-plan-at-a-time process, Broderick did not appear to consider any alternatives to his plan of "waiting for ground truth." In his testimony, he never claimed to have formally considered other options, such as "wait until I have three reports of levee breaches." Nor did he lay out the pros and cons of his chosen plan versus others. Throughout his testimony, he argued that his plan was to inform others only when he had ground truth.

As Monday progressed, Broderick was unable to get clear confirmation either way. He felt very frustrated. He clearly had a strong emotional tag telling him to get confirmed information, but he was not able to get what he wanted. Moreover, he did not articulate exact criteria for what constituted "confirmed information." As with beauty, he would recognize it when he saw it. He would rely on his unconscious pattern recognition processes to help him distinguish between ground truth and other reports.

By 6:00 p.m. he felt he had what he needed: a statement from FEMA that it could cope, a statement from the Army Corps of Engineers that it had not identified any breaches, and the reports on CNN of the party in Bourbon Street at which locals were claiming that they had dodged the bullet. Why did he give more credence to these pieces of information than to the other seventeen or so reports of breached levees and significant flooding?

The sources and the type of information fit with Broderick's experience of ground truth: his unconscious pattern recognition process told him that these were more significant bits of information than the other reports. One was from an army source. Being a marine, he may have had more faith in information from army sources. One was personal and vivid: the CNN report. Personal experiences tend to have stronger emotional tags than other types of data. One was from the FEMA "commander on the ground." In the Marines, Broderick would have learned not to interfere with the soldier on the ground, without very strong evidence.

Broderick felt he finally had the confirming information he needed. So situation report 7 stated that the levees had not been breached. He then went home, no doubt much relieved.

At this critical point, Broderick seems again to have followed the one-plan-at-a-time process. We found no evidence that he seriously considered alternatives to the report or that he convened a major meeting in the operations center to debate the balance of information that had come in that day. The analytical and emotional parts of his brain were telling him that he had the confirmed information he had been looking for all day.

Broderick's behavior is a good illustration of both the way in which our thinking is influenced by pattern recognition and emotional tags as well as the difficulty we have in challenging our thoughts so that we can spot and correct errors. Even on Tuesday morning, with significantly more evidence suggesting major levee breaches and an additional twelve hours for reflection, Broderick was still influenced by his earlier situation assessment: that this was a bad hurricane with significant flooding but no catastrophe. It was not until he had a direct report from the Army Corps of Engineers that he altered his point of view.

Broderick, of course, was making decisions under significant time pressure and with little opportunity to check the information he was receiving. Most significant decisions allow more time for reflection and more opportunity to get ground truth. Nevertheless, our thinking processes are still open to error. The extra time for reflection and checking does not eliminate the root causes of thinking errors. In the next chapter, which we devote to pattern recognition, we will share an example where a pattern recognition error by a French astronomer lasted for sixteen years.

TWO

Pattern Recognition

I N 1994, QUAKER WAS a successful and expanding food company. It had been well led by CEO William D. Smithburg since 1981. But Smithburg was about to make his biggest mistake: the acquisition of Snapple, the leading producer of iced tea and fruit juice drinks. Indeed, the acquisition proved to be disastrous. It led directly to Smithburg and Quaker's downfall. Just three years later, Snapple was divested to the Triarc Company for some $1.4 billion less than the purchase price (or at 18¢ on the dollar). Not long after that, Smithburg retired. Quaker itself was acquired by PepsiCo in 2000.

The roots of this decision went back to Smithburg's experience in the successful acquisition of Gatorade, a sports drink company, in 1983. Of all of Smithburg's initiatives, this single acquisition proved to be the most successful. As he told us, "We virtually built [Gatorade] from scratch."[1] The success of Gatorade transformed the performance of Quaker.

The logic behind the Snapple acquisition was to repeat this success story with another drinks company that, like Gatorade when Quaker acquired it, was successful in its niche but underexploited. In the words of Don Uzzi, Quaker's beverage division president at the time of the acquisition: "We have an excellent sales and marketing team here at Gatorade. We believe we do know how to build brands, we do know how to advance businesses. And our expectation is that we will do the same as we take Snapple as well as Gatorade to the next level."[2]

Quaker management saw Snapple as a high-potential brand, like Gatorade a decade earlier, and believed that the marketing expertise that made Gatorade explode into a megabrand could be applied to Snapple. As Smithburg explained, "The Snapple acquisition was predicated on two assumptions. First, that we could stem the decline in the brand with marketing, and second, that there would be great synergies with Gatorade. Unfortunately, neither of these worked out."[3]

In reality, the experience with Gatorade proved to be highly misleading. On the face of it, Snapple looked similar, with a similar potential for expansion, improving the brand, and brand extension. But there were important differences. For example, whereas Gatorade had been a clear category leader on the rise, Snapple was a category leader in trouble. Competitors had entered its market and taken share. Its growth was slowing, not accelerating, even prior to the acquisition. And there were other differences. At Gatorade, the management team stayed with the business after the deal. All but one of the top team at Snapple moved on. At Gatorade, operations were in good shape. At Snapple, inventory and production were out of control. The business lost $75 million in 1995, with a 5 percent decline in sales to $640 million.

The differences between Gatorade and Snapple went deeper. Snapple was an "image" drink, while Gatorade was a "fluid replacement product"; Snapple's success to that point was based on quirky marketing that created a cult following, while Gatorade was aggressively segmented and promoted in a more traditional fashion; Snapple relied on entrepreneurial distributors, while Gatorade used a warehouse system. As former Triarc CEO Michael Weinstein told us, "Quaker believed the Gatorade model could be applied to Snapple, but this just scared the system. Smithburg never got it."[4] When Quaker tried to "Gatorize" Snapple, it disregarded Snapple's tribal knowledge about customers, distribution channels, and product promotion in favor of its own set of beliefs on how to sell a bottled drink.

Yet Smithburg was a veteran of the food and drink industry, and Uzzi was a drinks expert who had watched Snapple create the fruit drink sector. How could they have got it so wrong? Why didn't they spot the fact that Snapple was a different, more quirky, more entrepreneurial organization and avoid the acquisition, or at least keep the business separate until they had sorted out the operational problems?

Gaps in the Pattern

To explain this type of judgment failure, we need to understand more about pattern recognition. There are three aspects of pattern recognition we need to understand. First, pattern recognition is incredibly complex, involving many parts of the brain. Second, our brain makes guesstimates and fills in gaps based on experience. This allows us to function with incomplete information. And let's face it: if we had to wait until we had all the information, most decisions would be too slow—with potentially fatal consequences. That is why pattern recognition is a great friend to decision makers. It allows us to make (mostly) good judgments without being in possession of all the information. Third, most of the work our brain does during pattern recognition is unconscious. We recognize something or we don't. We do not know how we have arrived at the recognition, which parts of our brain have been involved, and what guesstimates have been made.

These three features—the assembly of interpretations from many different parts of the brain, the filling in of gaps to produce an understanding, and the fact that most of it happens unconsciously—work well for us most of the time. But they are not foolproof. We can make mistakes.

One problem comes from misinterpreting inputs. Because we recognize inputs by matching them with past experiences, we can easily misinterpret situations we are unfamiliar with. So, for example, Smithburg may have misinterpreted Snapple's leadership position as a strength to build on, as it had been at Gatorade. As it turned out, it was a mixed blessing. Having created the category, Snapple was losing share.

The second problem is that we can make errors when we fill in the gaps. Uzzi did not know all that he needed to know about the culture of Snapple. But his brain probably "presumed" that Snapple's culture was similar to that of Gatorade or that the differences were not important to the success of the business.

Neither of these problems would be so great if Smithburg and Uzzi were aware of the possible errors in all of their assessments. As new information arrived, it would be easy to check it against earlier assessments and adjust the overall judgment accordingly. Unfortunately, because most processing is unconscious, we are normally not aware of the steps of recognition or gap filling that have influenced our judgments. This makes it hard for us to audit our own thinking and adjust it. Smithburg and Uzzi had a point of view, and the rational side of their brain gave them reasons for their point of view. But the process that generated the point of view was much more complicated and more open to error than their rational reasoning implied. When new information comes in, it is likely to be assessed against rational reasoning rather than the audit trail of pattern recognition.

The better informed the pattern recognition process is, the smaller the gaps that have to be filled in and the more likely we are to avoid mistakes. So, for example, when we are experienced and expert, our pattern recognition makes the right interpretation and judgment effortlessly, allowing us to make contact with a tennis ball coming at us with topspin doing fifty miles per hour, and send it back to a point, no bigger than a bucket, twenty meters away. But change the composition of the tennis ball or the altitude of the tennis court (balls fly farther and bounce higher at higher altitudes) without warning, and we look foolish as our racket passes over or under the ball by a big margin. Smithburg and Uzzi's foolishness may have been caused by little more than a failure to recognize the different conditions.

Out on a Limb

Using functional magnetic resonance imaging (fMRI) scanners, neuroscientists have tracked the electrical signals in our brain to try to understand what is happening as we consider situations or make decisions.

Pattern recognition, it turns out, is a huge challenge for the brain. Even for relatively simple tasks like sight, many parts of the brain light up. And the flow is not just one way to a central synthesizing point; there is an interaction between different parts of the brain as recognition and interpretation take place. We have evolved powerful processes for helping us with this complex task.

V. S. Ramachandran is the world's leading expert on phantom limbs. He is director of the Center for Brain and Cognition and a professor at the Salk Institute, in La Jolla, California. His work with people who have lost limbs or lost the use of limbs has caused him to search for explanations for recurring experiences his patients have had. Some continue to feel limbs that are no longer there, for example. Others deny the existence of a limb that has been paralyzed or believe that they are using a limb that is not working.

To understand how this happens, Ramachandran has delved into the workings of the mind. In his book *Phantom in the Brain*, he describes the nature of the challenge of sight. To create an electrochemical version of what we are seeing, we must absorb a large amount of fragmented information about the environment. To do this, about thirty different parts of the brain work in parallel to create a "best guess" of what we are seeing—each focusing on a different aspect of what we see, such as color, edges, and movement. We then compare each aspect with our memories. Because anything we see is always a bit different from any past memory, we have to make complex comparisons of different patterns.

Ramachandran concludes: "This means that the primary visual cortex, far from being a mere sorting office for information coming in from the retina, is more like a war room where information is constantly being sent back from scouts, the brain is constantly enacting all sorts of scenarios, and then information is sent back up again to those same higher areas where the scouts are working. There's a dynamic interplay between the brain's so-called early visual areas and the higher visual centers, culminating in a sort of virtual reality simulation of (what we are looking at)."[5]

In other words, the first step in decision making—using pattern recognition (of which vision is a relatively well-researched example)—is a complex challenge that relies on multiple parts of the brain each using a matching process to make sense of the inputs. Ramachandran's description about pattern recognition can be applied to the Snapple example. As he considered whether Snapple was a good company to acquire, Smithburg's brain was operating a mini war room, absorbing data from many sources and trying to put it all together to form a coherent picture. Ramachandran suggests "that you create your own 'reality' from mere fragments of information, that what you 'see' is a reliable—but not always accurate—representation of what exists in the world."

Checkmate on Reality

Our ability to create "our own reality" is illustrated by figure 2-1. In the picture, one square is marked A and another B. Which square has the darker shading?

Your judgment, if it is the same as ours, is that square A has the darker shading. However, we are wrong. Both squares have the same shading. You will find this hard to believe because your pattern recognition process is telling you that B is lighter. What is more, you have a positive emotional tag to this judgment—of course B is lighter!

In reality, both A and B have the same shading. If you want to prove this to yourself, then photocopy this page, cut out the two squares, and put them side by side, or fold the page so that both squares are next to each other.

So what is happening? Why has pattern recognition let us down? It is because our pattern recognition processes are not about identifying exact matches, but rather using similarities and knowledge to arrive at interpretations. We recognize the black-and-white checkerboard. We note that square B is lighter than the squares next to it. Hence we conclude that B is a white square. Now, since B is a white square and A is a

FIGURE 2-1

Which is darker—A or B?

Source: Http://web.mit.edu/persci/people/adelson/checkershadow_illusion.htm. © 1995, Edward H. Adelson.

black square, B must be lighter than A. So we see B as lighter than A. In scientific terms, we have created our own reality.

We then find it almost impossible to see that the two squares have the same shading, because the process of creating our own reality involves making a permanent change in our stored (and storied) memories. Researchers have found that once someone has recognized a pattern, they will always instantaneously recognize the same pattern, even if the picture is shown to them months or even years later. There appears to be a long-term change in the connections between a few of the brain's 100 billion neurons that makes the pattern easy to recognize again.[6] The experience imprints itself on our neurons and influences how we interpret situations in the future. Hence we are partly influenced by previous imprints from seeing other checkerboards and partly influenced by the initial imprint from seeing this picture. The combination of imprints leaves us powerless in our attempt to see that the two squares have the same shading.

This research can be applied to the Snapple situation. It seems highly likely that Smithburg's brain was "imprinted" with an ability to recognize a Gatorade-type situation: a category leader in a fast-growth niche with potential for further development. Some of Smithburg's neurons would have been permanently changed so that he could more readily see this pattern. When he learned that Snapple was for sale, he may have immediately recognized it as another Gatorade. He may have been just as convinced that Snapple represented another Gatorade as you are convinced that square B has a lighter shade than square A.

Unconscious Processes

A second discovery from neuroscience is that pattern recognition occurs mainly unconsciously.

A powerful example of this is the case of Diane Fletcher. Diane suffered from severe carbon monoxide poisoning and was partly blinded as a result. She could recognize colors and textures but not shapes—not even her husband's face or her own reflection in a mirror. Dr. David Milner, a specialist in visual problems, conducted some standard visual tests on Diane. She was clearly blind. At one point he held up a pencil and asked Diane, "What's this?" He describes her surprising response: "As usual, Diane looked puzzled. Then she did something unexpected. 'Where, let me see it,' she said, reaching out and deftly taking the pencil from my hand."[7]

Dr. Milner was stunned. Diane's fingers had moved swiftly and accurately toward it, grasped it, and carried it back to her lap in one fluid motion. How had she been able to take the pencil so deftly from him, if she could not see it? Neuroscientists have concluded that our vision is part conscious, part unconscious. In some patients, such as Diane Fletcher, most of the conscious sight is gone. This is why she says and experiences that she is blind. But she retains parts of her vision that operate at an unconscious level. In fact, she is quite good at catching a ball—though she claims not to be able to see it.[8]

The message from this research and many other studies like it is that unconsciously we are capable of understanding things that our conscious brain is unable or unwilling to.[9] Consciousness allows us to reflect on something and evaluate it more carefully, but there is limited capacity in the cerebral cortex to do this. Hence most of the memory searching and pattern recognition goes on unconsciously.[10] What is more, the unconscious processes can make assessments for us and can direct our actions just as effectively as the conscious processes.

Don Uzzi's assessments about the situation at Snapple involved large volumes of unconscious processing of input. These surfaced into his consciousness in the form of synthesized recognitions. In the same way that you are able to recognize the checkerboard or the shading of the squares, he recognized an organization similar to Gatorade. Conscious thought can then act to alter or reassess these unconscious recognitions—but it takes effort. It also takes awareness of how the unconscious brain works and a willingness to accept that the initial judgment may be flawed. This is hard to do. It is easier and more natural to assume that what you recognize is real, especially when you have a good deal of experience. Uzzi, did not adjust his thinking until it was too late.

Mercury Rising

The unconscious processes we have described can trip up even the most rational and analytical mind. Urbain Leverrier was a French astronomer who died in 1877. He became famous as a result of his role in the discovery of the planet Neptune. Leverrier had been working on the problem of the orbit of the planet Uranus. It did not fit completely with the orbit that was predicted by Newtonian mechanics.

Leverrier was a painstaking analyst. He recalculated the orbit of Uranus by reexamining the data. It involved years of careful calculations, and he found a number of errors had been made by previous astronomers. However, his new calculations still did not fit with Newtonian mechanics.

Some astronomers were suggesting that Newton's inverse square law might not work in the farther reaches of space. So Leverrier set about considering all the possible explanations for the orbit. He concluded, after considering and rejecting several hypotheses, that Uranus's odd orbit was due to the existence of another planet, located farther away from the sun. Leverrier then set about predicting the orbit of this other planet.

Initially, he could not persuade the French or British observatories to look for this planet. He finally persuaded Galle and d'Arrest, astronomers in Berlin, to look. It only took a few days. Once Leverrier had given Galle and d'Arrest the coordinates, based on his painstaking predictions, they soon spotted the new planet. The discovery of Neptune was announced on September 25, 1846.

The sighting was quickly confirmed by other observatories, and at the age of thirty-five, Leverrier became a celebrity. His work was praised throughout his profession, with some even comparing him to Newton. Claude Flammarion, a famous French astronomer, wrote, "He discovered a star with the tip of his pen, without other instruments than the strength of his calculations alone."[11] So far, so good. But what happened next is a good example of how pattern recognition can lead even the brightest people astray. About fifteen years later, Leverrier announced the existence of yet another planet. He had noticed a peculiarity in the orbit of Mercury that could not be explained by Newtonian mechanics. Using the methodology he had applied to the Uranus orbit, he had needed nearly thirteen years of calculations to conclude that another planet existed inside the orbit of Mercury—closer to the sun than Mercury.

Again he provided coordinates of where the planet could be found. This time it took nearly three months before Edmonde Lescarbault, an amateur astronomer, claimed to have seen the planet. Lescarbault's sighting was not as a result of the coordinates Leverrier had issued. Lescarbault claimed that he had sighted the planet by chance some months before Leverrier issued his guidance. As a result, Leverrier visited Lescarbault to check the authenticity of his sighting. Although

Lescarbault's instruments were poor and his recordings somewhat incomplete, Leverrier confirmed that the planet had been found, and named it Vulcan.

Again his discovery was treated as a triumph. The main observatories, eager to confirm the finding, requested new coordinates and timings. Leverrier readily complied, but no sightings were made. He redid his calculations and offered new coordinates and timings. Still no sightings were made. Nevertheless, Leverrier continued to believe in the existence of Vulcan. He issued new coordinates and timings almost every year until his death in 1877. By then, most of the scientific community no longer believed in Vulcan or any other planet between Mercury and the sun. In fact, it was not until 1915 and Einstein's theory of relativity that the peculiarities of the orbit of Mercury were fully explained.

So why did this painstaking analyst not see, like all other astronomers, that because no planet could be found, it probably did not exist? Because the situation was so similar to one he recognized, both consciously and unconsciously. Because his "discovery" of Vulcan was similar to his discovery of Neptune, his mind kept telling him that it was real, in the same way as Smithburg's mind kept telling him that Snapple was another Gatorade, or your mind is probably still telling you that square B is lighter than square A.

How We Fill Gaps

Another finding from brain research is that to make an assessment or to recognize something, we fill the gaps in the information we have. Moreover, because we do this unconsciously, we are not aware of the assumptions we have made.

This is easy to demonstrate. We all have a blind spot—a point on the retina where the optic nerve joins the eye. Looking at figure 2-2, if you close your right eye, fix the other eye on the circle symbol on the right side of the page, and move the page back and forward, the cross on the left side of the page eventually disappears. When you focus one eye on

FIGURE 2-2

the circle, your blind spot is aimed at the remaining symbol; so you cannot see it, even though you know it is there. Our brain takes in this information and, using experience, judges that the area of the page not observable due to the blind spot is likely to be white, just like its surroundings. So our visual process communicates "white space" to our conscious mind, and the cross disappears. Unfortunately, even if we know that our interpretation is wrong (as we do with the cross), we can't help ourselves.[12] We still see a blank.

The ability of the brain to deceive some of V. S. Ramachandran's patients goes far beyond this simple example. In one case, he reports, "An amateur athlete lost his arm in a motorcycle accident but continues to feel a phantom arm with vivid sensations . . . He can 'touch' things and even reach out and 'grab' a coffee cup. If I pull the cup away from him suddenly, he yelps in pain. 'Ouch! I can feel it being wrenched from my fingers,' he says wincing."[13]

Ramachandran concludes that the brain creates these peculiar "realities" for his patients because it is trying to use experience to explain what is going on. It is filling in the gaps in the situation and creating a reality that is as close a fit as the brain can imagine based on experience. Because the process happens unconsciously, the patients are unaware that what they see or feel is "foolish."

Leverrier's foolishness over Vulcan seems quite mild compared with believing that it hurts when a coffee cup is wrenched away from a hand that you no longer have—but it is generated by similar mental processes. As our mind tries to make sense of the world, it can make mistakes that cause us to think erroneous thoughts or behave in odd ways.

The Wisdom of Tennis

Even so, as we have pointed out with the tennis shot example, our pattern recognition skills are remarkable. When we have the appropriate experience, we can assess situations and decide what to do faster than the speed of a tennis ball. In fact, we can go through the whole process without much conscious thought at all.

But when we are new to the situation, we can get it very wrong. You only have to watch someone who has never played tennis before—flailing about, standing in the wrong place, swinging at the wrong time, and sending the ball to the wrong part of the court—to realize this. We are all capable of mistakes when faced with unfamiliar conditions. However, inexpert tennis players know they are getting it wrong. They have ample data to tell them that their technique is not working. Much of the time, however, it is not so easy for us to see that our judgment is flawed. In fact, we are most at risk of making bad decisions when we have enough experience to believe that we are right.

It is the expert tennis player fooled by an unfamiliar change in altitude, ball composition, court surface, or racket length that we are most interested in. Because our pattern recognition depends on input-matching and gap-filling processes that work well when we have sufficient relevant experience, we can be caught out because we think we have sufficient experience in situations when we do not. We can believe we are being wise when we are being foolish. Like Smithburg or Leverrier, we can hit at the ball with full confidence, only to find that we have missed it by a wide margin.

This propensity for error is easy to observe in a fast, real-time game, like tennis. But does it have the same consequences in major decisions that often take months of analysis and debate? The answer is that it can, even for world experts. The Snapple acquisition decision and execution took almost a year. Leverrier worked on the aberrations of Mercury's orbit for thirteen years, and then, after the amateur sighting of Vulcan, continued to provide orbit calculations and debate the issue with the world's best astronomers for another sixteen years. In other words, we are all at risk from erroneous pattern recognition, even for those decisions we take most care over. As a result, we need to identify when it may occur and put in place some defenses to reduce the risk that we will make flawed judgments.

Red Flags in Pattern Recognition

Our risk of flawed pattern recognition is greatest under two of the red flag conditions we have identified: when we have misleading experiences or misleading prejudgments.

Misleading experiences are memories, like Smithburg's Gatorade memory, that seem similar to the situation we are assessing, but are not. Our unconscious mind believes it has made a pattern match and informs our conscious mind that this is a situation we recognize. It then fills the conscious mind with the implications of this recognition. Whether it is a face, a tennis ball, a potential acquisition target, or a set of mathematical calculations, our conscious and subconscious start to react on assumptions derived from the recognized experience. As we will see in the next chapter, our mind also accesses the emotions linked to memories of this previous experience. If the experience we are linking to is misleading, we are likely to make flawed judgments about the real situation and believe that our flawed judgments are sound. (Chapter 5 is devoted to misleading experiences.)

Misleading prejudgments are previous decisions or judgments that mislead current judgments. These previous judgments could be viewed as a different form of previous experience, because they are often associated with previous experiences. However, because many of our prejudgments are taught to us rather than learned from experience and because we can make decisions and judgments without any relevant experience, it is useful to have two categories of misleading memory: misleading experiences and misleading prejudgments. (Chapter 6 is devoted to misleading prejudgments.)

Prejudgments can be rules of thumb that have been influencing the individual for years. For example, Don Uzzi may have used a rule of thumb that it was important to do most of the hard work of postmerger integration in the first one hundred days after the deal is closed: a common piece of advice from textbooks on postmerger integration. Unfortunately, in the Snapple case, this would have been misleading.

Prejudgments can also be earlier judgments or decisions made in connection with the current situation. Having judged that Snapple was similar to Gatorade, Smithburg and Uzzi would have found it much harder to spot differences as they got to know the new business better. Their prejudgment would have misled their natural pattern recognition processes. Leverrier's judgment that Vulcan had been spotted by Lescarbault misled him into misreading the signals he was getting from other astronomers that Vulcan did not exist. In fact, for Leverrier, the combination of the experience of using Newton's laws to discover Neptune, and the judgment that Lescarbault had spotted Vulcan, appears to have misled him until his death.

Armed with an understanding of how our pattern recognition processes can be misled, we are in a much stronger position to anticipate situations when our brains may get it wrong. This makes it possible for us to strengthen the process we use to make certain decisions. If we can identify when our thinking might be at risk from misleading experiences or misleading prejudgments, we can take steps to protect ourselves. By involving other people, collecting additional data, insisting on thorough debate, or even just being aware of our own fallibility, we can reduce the risk of making a flawed decision. But as we shall see in the next chapter, our brains are not only affected by pattern recognition errors. Our thinking can also be distorted by our emotions.

THREE
___

Emotional Tagging

A<small>N WANG FOUNDED</small> Wang Laboratories in 1951. By the early 1980s, it had become one of the most successful computer companies in the world.

Wang Labs succeeded because of innovations led by An Wang, such as the magnetic core memory—a phototypesetting device that increased the productivity of news printing—and one of the first electronic calculators. Wang's most successful product, however, was its word processor. Launched in 1976, the Wang 120 WPS stored information and allowed the user to edit text. It made the electric typewriter obsolete almost overnight. It catapulted Wang Labs forward, and, importantly, it hurt IBM in a core business.

By the early 1980s, Wang Labs was in a strong position to exploit the electronic developments and the distributed processing trend that were to dominate in the next ten years. With sales of only $3 billion, compared with IBM's $47 billion, An Wang set the ambitious target of overtaking IBM as the leading computer company by 1990. For the next few years, he carried around in his top pocket a scorecard charting his progress against IBM. Unfortunately, the result was not glory, but bankruptcy in the early 1990s.

The decision that started the demise of Wang Labs was An Wang's reluctance to develop a personal electronic computer. Early models from Atari were showing promise, and Apple was the technical leader. Yet Wang rejected the opportunity, commenting, "The PC is the stupidest thing I ever heard of."[1] As a result, Wang was slow to market with the 1980s killer app.

This decision was surprising. Wang had already made important inventions. The personal electronic computer was not technically beyond the company. Moreover, the impetus for developing a PC at Wang came from an influential source—his son Fred, and it was Fred who gave us insights into his father's thinking.

When IBM entered the market in 1981 with the 5150 PC, which was reasonably priced and ran with a nonproprietary operating system, the market began to explode. Four months after the 5150 was introduced, it was named *Time*'s Man of the Year. Wang could no longer ignore the market. But he then made another bad decision. He chose a proprietary operating system at a time when the rest of the industry was going IBM compatible. The Wang personal computer was not an immediate disaster, but it left Wang Labs competitively exposed. As customers replaced word processors with computers, Wang's fortunes declined rapidly.

While An Wang was not the only business leader who made wrong calls during this turbulent period,[2] those close to him believe that the main drivers behind these mistakes were his emotions. First, he was reputed to be "in love" with the Wang word processor. His feelings for the product went far beyond pride and commercial enthusiasm. He felt as proud and protective as a parent. This made it hard for him to embrace the technology that would make the word processor obsolete. Second, he hated IBM. Not only was IBM his target competitor; he felt he had been cheated and exploited by the company in his early career over a technology licensing deal. Hence he was reluctant to consider supporting a product platform that had been developed by IBM.

An Wang no doubt wanted to do the right thing for his company, and he was probably highly logical and consistent in his arguments. Nevertheless, the factor guiding his judgments was most likely his emotions: his love of the word processor and his hatred of IBM.

In this chapter we will explain why emotions play such a big part in decision making. In fact, we will argue that without emotions, we are unable to make decisions at all. Armed with this understanding, we will explain how emotions can be a two-edged sword, both helping us make brilliant decisions and fooling us into flawed decisions.

Military Maneuvers

In his book *On the Psychology of Military Incompetence*, Norman Dixon, a soldier turned professor of psychology, describes a number of military campaigns in which the leader and his team pigheadedly stuck to a flawed plan, despite mounting evidence that disaster was looming.

One of the most striking of Dixon's examples is that of Operation Market Garden, the Allies' attempt to use paratroops to capture three river bridges in the Netherlands, and send ground forces across them to outflank the German army and end the Second World War in Europe.

The Allied landings in Normandy in June 1944 had resulted by late August in the destruction of two German armies in France, and intelligence suggested that they had few reserves left in the field. The Allies had strong forces available but limited supplies, so Field Marshal Montgomery wanted to concentrate the Allies' logistical efforts on supporting a single strong thrust in the north to exploit the Germans' disarray before they had a chance to recover. His plan was for three airborne divisions to capture the three bridges, and an armored corps to drive its way up the resulting 64-mile "airborne corridor" to enter the north German plain. The first two bridges were at Grave and Nijmegen, and the third spanned the Rhine River at Arnhem. Montgomery's boss, General Eisenhower, wanted to advance more steadily on a broad front, but allowed Market Garden to go ahead.

The plan was bold and high risk. The airborne landings needed good weather over several days, as there were not enough aircraft to deliver all the paratroopers in one lift. The airborne troops were lightly armed, so it was critical that the ground forces move quickly, or the paratroopers could be overrun. The plan set the ground forces a target of reaching the farthest bridge at Arnhem in seventy-two hours. They had to advance up a single narrow road intersected with difficult, marshy land on either side. The Germans would only need to block the front of this column to impose serious delays. The Allies' superior numbers would be of no use. The impassable nature of the marshy ground on either side of the road meant that only the front of the Allied force would be able to engage the enemy. Delay would give the Germans the chance to bring up sufficient reserves to overwhelm the airborne bridgeheads. Everything had to go right—either failure to capture any one of the bridges or delays to the ground forces' advance would condemn the plan to failure.

The airborne forces were led by Lieutenant General "Boy" Browning. A veteran of the First World War, he was eager to command troops in action before the war ended. He had built up the British airborne forces from the beginning, and Market Garden would be the biggest airborne operation in history. He wanted to be part of it. The paratroopers were an elite force that had spearheaded the invasion of Normandy. They were restless. Market Garden was their chance. The risks seemed acceptable.

On September 15, two days before Market Garden was due to be launched, new intelligence suggested that two SS panzer divisions were refitting in and around Arnhem. If so, this force could easily block the advancing ground troops and potentially prevent the capture of the third bridge. The commander of the British First Airborne Division, which was due to land there, rushed to see Browning, only to be treated "as a nervous child suffering from a nightmare."[3] When his intelligence officer showed Browning aerial photographs of the German tanks, Browning told the officer, "I wouldn't trouble myself about these if I were you . . . they're probably not serviceable at any rate."[4] A medic was then sent to examine the intelligence officer. The medic advised the officer to take some leave because he was obviously exhausted. The information was ignored.

The mission went ahead, initially taking the Germans by surprise. But then the weather broke, delaying the dropping of airborne reinforcements and supplies and depriving the Allied troops on the ground of air support. Despite unexpectedly strong resistance, the paratroopers captured the bridges at Grave and Nijmegen but only took one end of the bridge at Arnhem. However, the problem was with the ground forces. After nine days of hard fighting, they had still not gotten through to the Arnhem bridge. Reluctantly, the paratroopers had to be withdrawn and the campaign abandoned. The cost had been high. The First Airborne had lost some 60 percent of its strength. As the well-known historian Max Hastings recently summed it up, "Market Garden was a rotten plan, poorly executed."[5]

Why were the commanding officers so resistant to information that the Germans had additional forces? Professor Dixon blames emotions. "The apparent intellectual failings of some military commanders are due not to lack of intelligence but to their feelings," he writes.[6] Browning was attached to the airborne concept and was desperate to prove it by getting his men into action.[7] Doing so was clearly in his personal interests. One of his contemporaries labeled the operation "Operation KCB" in reference to a belief that Browning's main motivation was to win a knighthood, which he indeed received.[8]

Montgomery, who was normally cautious and very careful not to bite off more than his forces could chew, might have acted as a counterbalancing voice of reason. But he was angered by Eisenhower's initial opposition to his idea of a single thrust and so became very attached to Market Garden, ridiculing those who challenged it. Had it been a success, he stood to reestablish his prominence among the Allied commanders and possibly be the man who ended the war by Christmas. In the words of Max Hastings, "[Montgomery's] motives do not seem hard to read. Bitterly chastened by his removal from the allied ground command, he was determined to sustain the primacy of his own role in the battle for Germany. In consequence, he focused his entire attention on the issue of how the enemy's front might be broken in Holland, where the British stood. He displayed no interest in other opportunities further south, on the front of Bradley's US 12th Army Group . . . Montgomery's jealousy of Eisenhower affected his decisions at every stage."[9]

Those involved in planning Market Garden were highly intelligent and competent, as their records elsewhere show. In this case, their hearts ruled their heads at huge cost to those involved.

The Iowa Gambling Task

Antonio Damasio, one of the world's leading researchers in neuroscience, helped design a seminal experiment assessing the role of emotions in decision making. It is known as the Iowa Gambling Task.[10] The experiment was first conducted at the University of Iowa, College of Medicine, when Damasio was head of the Department of Neurology.

The experiment works as follows. Participants are seated at a table on which four decks of cards have been placed. The players are given $2,000 in play money and told that the object of the task is to make money. Some cards, they are told, will give them a payout—as much as $100—while others have penalties, sometimes several hundred dollars. They can choose cards from any pile.

What the players do not know is that the gains and losses from two decks—the bad decks—are negative. While those from the other decks—the good decks—are positive. Each deck has different cards, with different payouts and penalties. The bad decks, on average, offer higher payouts but even higher penalties. If a player were to pick ten cards in a row from a bad deck, he would expect payouts of $1,000 and penalties of $1,250, leaving a net loss of $250. If the player were to pick ten cards from a good deck, the payout on average would be $500 and the losses $250, giving a net gain of $250.

The players are hooked up to equipment to detect emotional responses such as heart rate and skin conductance, both good measures of emotional arousal. They are also asked to explain what they are thinking as they draw cards.

At first, players draw cards randomly, noting the outcomes. However, as soon as a player draws a penalty card, the emotions, recorded by the electric monitors, start to become active. After a few cards, it is possible to observe greater emotional activity when players are about to choose cards from the bad decks, even before the players make any comments about these decks. In fact, players start to prefer the good decks and avoid the bad decks, before they are able to articulate what they are doing or why they are doing it. The explanation for their behavior usually comes twenty or so cards after their behavior starts to change and as much as thirty cards after their emotions are signaling that they have concerns about the bad decks.

The order of their responses is as follows. First they exhibit an emotional response to penalty cards. Then they exhibit emotional responses whenever they are drawing from the bad decks. Then they start to avoid the bad decks, without being aware that they are doing so. The process is clearly subconscious. The next stage is that they begin to articulate a preference for the good decks, without being able to say exactly why. They have a gut bias. Finally, players explain that they are avoiding the bad decks because the gains are consistently less than the penalties. From then on, they only draw from the good decks.

This experiment demonstrates that our emotions are part of our decision-making process. In fact, emotions appear to lead the process, even in an exercise that is as unemotional as drawing cards from decks. The order of the decision-making process appears to be as follows. The process starts with inputs from the environment: the information from the cards. The next step is an unconscious emotional reaction. This is followed by behavioral change in line with the emotional reaction. Then we become conscious of the feelings that are driving the behavioral change. These are our gut feelings. Finally, we are able to make a decision using a process of reasoning. Eventually, most players avoid the bad decks entirely and are able to give a rational explanation of the differences between the decks.[11]

It may seem odd that we can have feelings we are not aware of that can influence our behavior without our knowing it, and that our emotional judgments come often before our rational judgments. But it appears to be true. Damasio suggests that this brings considerable benefits. Emotion "focuses attention on certain aspects of the problem and thus enhances the quality of reasoning."[12] Doing so "narrows the decision-making space and increases the probability that the action will conform to past experience."[13]

Intrigued by the results of the Iowa Gambling Task, Damasio decided to see whether there was a different response from people who had suffered damage to parts of their brain that are responsible for generating and processing the emotions used in making decisions and, in particular, the ventromedial sector of the frontal cortex.[14] These people scored well on tests of intellect and were able to function quite normally, but their decision-making systems seemed to be impaired. They did not seem to be able to anticipate negative consequences.

While the players with damage to the prefrontal cortex did react when encountering a penalty card, they did not show any emotional anticipation when picking cards from the bad decks. Because they were not anticipating the negative outcome, they did not start to avoid the bad decks. In addition, they did not experience a hunch that the bad decks might be giving them a negative return.

What was even more fascinating was that some emotionally damaged players continued to pick cards from the bad decks even after they consciously understood what was going on and could lucidly explain the differences between the decks—which they were able to do at about the same point as the players without brain damage. Even after one hundred draws, they kept right on picking cards from the bad decks, despite their mounting losses.[15]

Damasio's conclusion is that because the emotions of these players could not influence the decision-making process, they were unable to make a decision to change their behavior. They could understand intellectually what was going on. But emotions seem to be necessary to turn that information into a decision that affects behavior.

Games of Tag

Damasio and others (including Daniel Goleman, the author of *Emotional Intelligence*) hypothesize that when the brain stores a memory of an event or action, it also stores an associated emotion with it.[16] This is what we call *emotional tagging*.[17]

When we find ourselves in a situation that requires us to make a decision, our brain (as part of the pattern recognition process described in the previous chapter) will recall past situations that seem similar to the current one, and access the emotions that are tagged to them. Players reaching toward a bad deck will engage the emotions they have experienced with this deck. If the previous emotions are negative overall, the player will exhibit negative emotions—signaled by a higher heart rate and sweaty palms—when taking a card from this deck. For example, when participants first consider which deck to pick from, they feel no particular emotions because they have no prior experience of either deck. However, as the experiment progresses, they begin to experience the higher levels of punishment associated with the bad deck. Their emotions begin to warn them against selecting from this deck. People with damage to the parts of the brain responsible for emotions or emotional tagging, however, do not feel such emotions and so continue to select from the bad deck.

Consider how this might have affected An Wang. He was deciding whether to develop a product to compete in the evolving personal computer market. This situation would be likely to cause him to think about the possible impact on word processors. His love for his most successful product would cause him to feel emotionally protective. His initial instinct probably would have been to look for ways of improving the word processor to protect it from any loss of sales.

He may also have recalled other situations where higher-end applications threatened a standard product. Since high-end products do not normally take significant share from the mass market, he may have felt comforted and decided that little action was needed. He may even have had a personal experience of trying to introduce a technically more sophisticated product in some other market, and experienced the negative emotions of failure. This combination of emotions may have been the driving force behind his reluctance to launch a personal computer and his comment that the personal computer was one of the stupidest ideas he had come across.

We are not suggesting that managers like An Wang are completely dominated by their emotions. But as the Iowa Gambling Task demonstrates, we are all influenced by our emotions, even when we are doing something as dull as drawing cards from decks.

Could An Wang have overcome these emotional influences and decided to enter the personal computer market much earlier than he did? The answer is yes. Our reasoning enables us to overrule our emotions. However, it can be difficult. Wang would probably have needed an input that engaged rival emotions, such as an impassioned plea from a colleague or a loyal customer rejecting the word processor for a personal computer.

As it turned out, he did change his mind. The success of personal computers started to hurt sales of word processors, and with the launch of the IBM PC, the threat from personal computers became much more vivid. We can suppose that his emotional fear of the growing sales of PCs became greater than his emotional reluctance to undermine sales of his word processors. So he decided to develop a personal computer product.

He then faced the decision of copying IBM or creating a proprietary operating program. Here, his bad feelings and long-standing competition with IBM were likely to have had an influence. These emotions were probably telling him not to play second fiddle to IBM. Other factors, of course, may have been involved. But the emotions would have been an influence, whether he was conscious of them or not. His final choice to develop a proprietary operating system may well have been justified based on a purely rational analysis of the options. However, those we spoke to felt he was overly influenced by his dislike of IBM.

Because strategic decisions are complex, there are normally crunch judgments that have to be made. For these judgments, reasoning and facts are typically not enough to prove the case one way or another. Instincts, gut feelings, and intuition, all of which rely on our emotional tags, are called on to help. Normally, these emotional tags help us make the right call, as they did for the players in the Iowa Gambling Task. However, on occasions they let us down.

An Wang would have relied partly on his gut feelings to judge the prospects of the PC market and then to assess the wisdom of aligning with IBM. Unfortunately, his emotional tags let him down. General Browning, faced with new intelligence about enemy forces, would have relied partly on his gut feelings to assess the importance of the aerial photographs. Again, his emotional tags let him down.

Emotions and Commitment

Emotional tags are not only relevant in the process of accessing past memory. We also need emotions to commit to a decision. We need commitment to act. We need confidence that we are doing the right thing and energy to see us through setbacks and difficulties. Hence we generate additional emotions in the act of deciding.

Question: Five birds are sitting on a log. Two decide to fly away. How many are left? The answer three probably comes to mind.

The correct answer, however, is five. Two birds *decided* to fly away, but that doesn't mean they actually did.

This riddle was a favorite of managers at the Royal Bank of Scotland (RBS), a large U.K. bank, after its takeover of National Westminster Bank (NatWest) in 2000. The RBS managers felt that an important reason for their company's success was its bias to action. They analyze a problem, quickly push to make a decision, and then move swiftly into execution. To RBS, "analysis paralysis" is a worse sin than acting quickly on a decision, even if the action needs to be adjusted later or has to be abandoned altogether. RBS managers used the riddle to encourage the NatWest people to make decisions and take actions. They wanted NatWest managers to understand that agreement to a choice is not enough to guarantee implementation. Action is required, and action requires emotional commitment.[18]

Antonio Damasio provides a good example of this. He describes a discussion with one of his brain-damaged patients: a man whose cognitive functions were intact but who had no ability to use his emotions when making decisions. The two were trying to schedule the patient's next appointment. Damasio suggested two possible dates. The patient embarked on an interminable, beautifully argued enumeration of the pros and the cons and the maybes of the different days. After some minutes, Damasio could listen no longer. He told the patient to visit on the second of the two dates. "That's fine," said the patient, as though there had never been any issue.[19]

Neuroscience has not yet, to our knowledge, found an explanation of exactly how emotions work to influence the commitment to action. However, it is likely that just as our decision making is focused and guided by emotional tags, emotions affect the level of commitment we have to action. If a selected action, and its projected outcome, has strong positive emotional tags, then we are likely to act more decisively. If we have conflicting emotions, then we are more likely to be ambivalent about the proposed action.

But the emotions for action do not come only from the emotional tags we already have. The process of deciding can generate its own emotions. As we get excited about the decision, we tag it with additional positive emotions. As we get reinforcement that we have made the right decision, this generates stronger emotional tags. This is probably what was behind General Browning's seemingly incompetent rejection of important intelligence. His commitment to the Arnhem plan had become so great that any threat to the plan generated a negative emotion. To avoid the negative emotion that would come from accepting the intelligence, his brain would have volunteered the idea that the intelligence might be wrong. This interpretation would have been tagged with a positive emotion because it supported the plan. In looking for reasons why the intelligence might be flawed, he would have looked for confirmatory evidence. Perhaps he noticed the intelligence officer's tired-looking eyes and built further positive emotions around this interpretation.

Researchers have a label for this kind of mental process: *cognitive dissonance*. Once we have made a judgment, we embrace confirming information and discount disconfirming information. We do this by giving confirming information a positive emotional tag and disconfirming information a negative tag. The result is that our mental processes give more weight to the confirming information.[20]

Emotional Power

So far we have demonstrated that emotions influence decisions and are generated by decisions. As we point out in the previous section and take further in the box "How Emotions Influence Decisions," decisions result from a blend of emotion and reasoning. However, sometimes emotions can take control. Sometimes emotions can dominate decision making.

HOW EMOTIONS INFLUENCE DECISIONS

For a long time scientists ignored the role played by emotions in decision making—preferring to treat every choice as a form of cognition. However, in the past few decades, the spotlight has turned back onto emotions. Neuroscientist Paul MacLean's model of the triune brain is an example. MacLean was a physician and scientist who held senior positions at Yale Medical School, Harvard University, and the National Institute of Mental Health. His work on the structure of the brain has been described as one of the most influential ideas in neuroscience over the past fifty years.

MacLean suggests that the brain can be split into three sections (see figure 3-1). Each comes from a different group of our ancestors. The oldest, reptilian section is our brain stem, responsible for managing the daily routines of life: heartbeat, respiration, reproduction, and defensive behaviors.

The next section of brain has evolved from our mammalian ancestors and is referred to as the limbic system. This section of the brain is responsible for memory and emotion. It contains the amygdala, responsible for managing fear, and the nucleus accumbens, responsible for managing pleasure.

FIGURE 3-1

Diagram of the brain

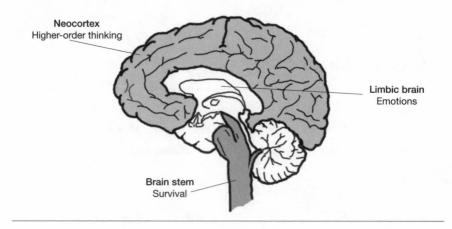

The most recently evolved and largest section of our brain, the neocortex, which we share with primates, is the part associated with consciousness and rationality.

MacLean's theory, which we have simplified here for clarity, suggests that our emotions come from a part of the brain quite different from that of our rational thinking.[21] Emotion and cognition appear to affect our behavior through different systems and processes and in very different ways. Emotions are more elemental. They provide the drives that motivate us. The reasoning part of our brain works in parallel, trying to harness, channel, and constrain the emotions. As Plato put it, we are sitting in a chariot drawn by two horses: reason and passion.

Emotions tend to be rather simple—either positive or negative. There may be relatively few pure emotions—anger, sadness, fear, and enjoyment, for example. These elemental feelings appear to be universal—specific facial expressions for fear, anger, sadness, and enjoyment—are recognized by people across diverse cultures. The richness of emotions comes from the fact that they can be combined, like primary colors. For example, jealousy may be a mix of anger and sadness. Guilt may be a combination of enjoyment and fear.[22]

Emotions are closely linked to action. In our mammalian past, they caused us to respond to food or to a predator. They do not require reflection. They encourage us to *do* something—whether it be to feed, fight, flee, or any of the other *f* words.[23] Emotions carry with them a sense of simplicity and clarity that makes action easier.[24]

Cognition has not developed as a way of taking action—that had already evolved with the reptilian and mammalian parts of the brain. Instead, cognition adds the ability to process data and to reflect. But without emotions, that is all that cognition is: an advanced data processing system, not a decision maker.

Emotions are powerful influences because they act at an unconscious level. Unconscious emotions have been shown to have a higher biasing effect on decisions than conscious feelings, presumably because the decision maker is less able to be reflective about the reasons for their choices.[25] Even if people are aware of their feelings, they are unlikely to be fully aware of the unconscious influence their feelings are having on their decision making.

There is some debate about the exact mechanisms through which emotions influence behavior. One theory is that emotions directly create a visceral response that changes behavior—much as one might imagine that an organism without consciousness would respond to a threat or an opportunity. Another theory is that emotions influence our cognitive processes and that the cognitive process then generates behavior. For example, Damasio believes that we can use emotional tags to guide our decision making without creating any changes in the rest of our body—unconscious emotions alert our cognitive brain directly. Indeed, Damasio thinks this is the most common way in which emotions affect decisions.

Probably both theories are true. An illustrative example is that of the fear response, which has been extensively researched by Joseph LeDoux. He describes how the sensory thalamus sorts incoming information and sends it in one of two directions. The "low road" sends signals directly to the amygdala, the part of the brain that initiates our fear responses. The "high road" sends signals first to the sensory cortex—where conscious and unconscious reasoning take place—and then to the amygdala to initiate action (see figure 3-2). These systems are working together, with a significant degree of feedback between them.

In LeDoux's model, emotions change behavior both directly and via our cognitive processes. In the low road, emotions act directly on the amygdala, which then initiates visceral and muscular changes. In the high road, the emotions act on the reasoning processes. The emotions act first—the low road is faster. They also provide a significant filtering of information and narrowing of options available to the reasoning brain.

How the interaction between emotion and cognition works is still at the frontier of neuroscience. However, emerging research suggests that raw emotions and reasoning operate together through complex systems, built up by linkages between different parts of the brain. Exactly which bits of the brain are involved for which emo-

FIGURE 3-2

LeDoux's view of the two pathways of the fear response

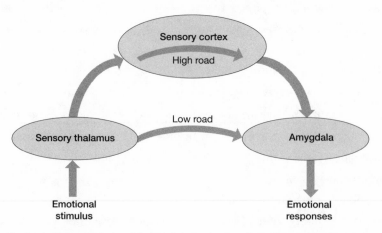

Source: Reprinted with the permission of Simon & Schuster, Inc. from The Emotional Brain: The Mysterious Underpinnings of Emotional Life by Joseph LeDoux. © 1996 by Joseph LeDoux.

tions, and how the emotional and cognitive, and conscious and unconscious, relate, is less clear.

It is our ability to moderate how we respond to our emotions that
Daniel Goleman cites as the key to emotional intelligence. As he describes it, "Ordinarily the complementarity of limbic system and
neocortex, amygdala and prefrontal lobes, means each is a full partner in mental life. When these partners interact well, emotional intelligence rises—as does intellectual ability."[26]

Laurence Gonzales, journalist and author, has been fascinated by
how people react in survival situations. In his riveting book, *Deep Survival*, Gonzales describes tens of stories of survival situations he has
researched.[27] In some, the people in the stories make the right decisions and survive. In many, they make the wrong decisions and die.

Gonzales uses Plato's analogy: "The human organism, then, is like a
jockey on a thoroughbred in the starting gate. He's a small man and it's
a big horse, and if it decides to get excited in that small metal cage, the
jockey is going to get mangled, possibly killed. So he takes great care to
be gentle. The jockey is reason and the horse is emotion, a complex of systems bred over eons of evolution and shaped by experience, which exist
for your survival. They are so powerful, they can make you do things
you'd never think to do, and they can allow you to do things you'd never
believe yourself capable of doing. The jockey can't win without the horse,
and the horse can't race alone."[28]

The horse is important. It has been a necessary part of our evolution.
We need the ability to make decisions and act without the intervention
of reason. It is this capability that enables us to drive on autopilot while
arguing with our spouse. Gonzales refers to Erich Maria Remarque's fic-
tionalized version of his actual experiences in World War I, *All Quiet on
the Western Front*: "At the sound of the first droning of the shells we rush
back, in one part of our being, a thousand years. By the animal instinct
that is awakened in us we are led and protected. It is not conscious: it
is far quicker, much more sure, less fallible, than consciousness. One

cannot explain it. A man is walking along without thought or heed—suddenly he throws himself down on the ground and a storm of fragments flies harmlessly over him—yet he cannot remember either to have heard the shell coming or to have thought of flinging himself down."

The thinking part of our brain takes too long to save us from shrapnel or from the pounce of a saber-toothed tiger. Hence our emotions are powerfully connected to our muscles and our viscera so that we do not have to wait for our much slower analytical thought processes.

Gonzales describes research he did among pilots on aircraft carriers. He was interested in the challenge it created for pilots: "that boundary between life and death, that place where, to stay alive, you have to remain calm and alert." He had chosen aircraft carriers because the navy had a long experience of the occasional young pilot who would fly his plane straight into the back of the aircraft carrier when trying to land. As a fellow pilot, Gonzales wanted to understand why. He chose the *Carl Vinson*, an American aircraft carrier in the Pacific Fleet:

Shortly before I arrived, one of the pilots was on final, heading toward the deck. He let his descent rate get away from him and got low and slow, and well . . . some would use the term panic, but that does not tell you much. There were plenty of sensory signals screaming at him that he'd better get on the power. All he had to do was move the hand on the throttle a few inches. The Landing Safety Officer had hit the pickle switch, activating those glaring red lights that mean You are not cleared to land! *The ball, an obvious light in a big Fresnel lens, was right in front of him, telling him he was low. And, of course, the Landing Safety Officer was yelling in his ear. Somehow none of it got through.*

The impact with the tail of the boat cut the plane in two, leaving the guy in the rear seat squashed like a bug on a windshield and sending the pilot skittering across the deck in a shower of sparks, still strapped into his Martin-Baker ejection seat.

The forces that cause a pilot to fly into the back of an aircraft carrier when every possible safety system is screaming at him or her are, according to Gonzales, the result of emotions that take control of us. As in vertigo, we are suddenly powerless. Our emotions are making direct connection with our actions and controlling us in the same manner that our breathing is controlled without thinking or that we flinch away from a sharp object.

Joseph LeDoux, a professor at New York University and a specialist in using animal research to understand the processes of fear and anxiety, is author of *The Emotional Brain*. He explains, "Conscious control over emotions is weak, but emotions can flood consciousness. This is because the wiring of the brain at this point in our evolutionary history is such that connections from the emotional systems to the cognitive systems are stronger than connections from the cognitive systems to the emotional systems."[29]

The fighter pilot, Gonzales proposes, will have experienced on a number of occasions the gut-gripping fear of coming in to land and the beautiful elation when the plane safely touches down. The amygdala, the source of fear-related emotions in the brain, will have been firing chemicals into the brain on the approach. It will have been screaming, "This is bad; we should do something to avoid it." The brain will have been searching for a memory of what to do in this situation. The strongest emotional memory will have been about how the danger goes away when the plane touches down. Hence the brain will have been sending messages to the body: "*Get the plane down.*" At the same time, the brain will have spotted the landing deck and will have recognized something it associates with pleasure. The nucleus accumbens, the part of the brain responsible for pleasure, will have been sending out chemicals, saying, "The deck is good; get to the deck; there is pleasure there." In other words, and to mix our transportation metaphors, all of the power of the horse was telling the pilot to get the plane down onto the deck.

Gonzales is able to be authoritative about pilots. On one occasion, as he was landing, his copilot had to punch him in the arm before Gonzales realized that the control tower was telling him he was on a collision course. He had not heard the control tower or seen the other plane. He had been so focused on the runway and getting his plane to land.

Most of the examples of emotions taking control are extreme situations where action needs to be taken quickly. Strategic decisions are rarely of this kind. They normally involve months of discussion and analysis. Hence we are unlikely to be completely overpowered by our emotions during this kind of decision. Nevertheless, it is important to be aware of the power of emotions. As with a real horse, we must recognize that, in certain conditions, it can run out of control.

Implications for Decision Making

Since emotions influence decisions, mainly in helpful ways, we do not want to try to eliminate their effect. In fact, because emotions mostly work on our body and unconscious, we could not eliminate their effect even if we tried.[30] Moreover, we need emotions to make decisions: we appear to be especially incompetent decision makers when the emotional part of our brain is damaged.

But emotions can sometimes lead us to disaster, so we need some way of anticipating when our emotions might be a problem. If we are forewarned, if we can identify potentially misleading emotional tags in advance, we can strengthen the decision process in ways that will help combat the influence of the emotion we are worried about.

For example, if we know that emotional tags can cause a pilot to continue to try to land even though he is already too low, we might want to install an ability for the landing safety officer to take control of the joystick and force the pilot to go around again. Or we might want to install electric shock equipment in the pilot's seat so that it is possible to jolt him out of his emotional trance.

Neither of these solutions is appropriate for the typical executive committee meeting or board of governors. But the thought process is the same. If we can anticipate when an emotion might distort the judgment of influential people, we can install some mechanism in the process that will help to combat the distortion.

We have identified four types of emotional tags that, if inappropriate, can interfere with sound decision making:

Intense emotional experiences. We may have powerful memories of successes, failures, fears, or pleasures that we experienced in the past. Most of the time, these emotions help us, as they did for Remarque's soldiers. But these emotional memories can also mislead us. Gonzales's pilot could not go around again, because his emotions were telling him to land the plane.

Previously made judgments and decisions. We can tag previous judgments and decisions with strong emotions. Where these judgments are sound, our emotions help us focus. But if the judgments are misleading, our emotions can cause us to cling to them long after others, less committed to these judgments, have seen the light. An Wang's statement that the "PC is the stupidest thing I ever heard of" reveals an emotional commitment to a judgment that contributed to his delay in launching a personal computer. General Browning's commitment to the attack on Arnhem appears to have clouded his judgment about the aerial photographs.

Personal interests. We often have personal interests at stake in the decisions we make. If these decisions only affect ourselves, our emotional tags will help us get to the right answer. But when our personal interests conflict with our responsibilities for other stakeholders, our judgment can be unbalanced. It is for this reason that members of a committee are often asked to leave the room or refrain from voting if they have a personal interest at stake. In the same way, politicians are expected to place their financial investments in the hands of an independent fund manager so that their judgments are not influenced by their personal gains or losses. In fact, the attention we give to incentives and aligning managers' interests with the interests of their organizations is recognition of the degree to which we think personal interests affect decisions.

Attachments. Since we are social animals, we are designed to become attached to other people. Love is a powerful emotion. But we can also become attached to a group or tribe, to places, and even to possessions. If the decision we are involved in is likely to affect one of our attachments, the emotions generated can unbalance our thinking. For example, An Wang's love of his word processor and hatred of IBM colored his thinking about the advantages of developing a personal computer.

The first two types of emotion add strength to the red flag conditions we identified in chapter 2. Intense emotional experiences, when inappropriate, are *misleading experiences* that can disrupt our pattern recognition processes. The stronger the emotions, the more likely they are to influence our thinking. In the same way, strong emotions attached to previous judgments can cause *misleading prejudgments* to dominate our thinking.

The other two types of emotion, however, suggest two additional red flag conditions: *inappropriate self-interest* and *inappropriate attachments*. As with the first two red flag conditions, we believe it is possible to spot their existence in advance of a decision and change the way the decision is made, to reduce the risk that they will distort the choice.

The reality is that emotions are interwoven into the decision-making process in ways that make them a necessary and important part of decision making. Much of their influence is unconscious, and we only become aware of them through our gut feelings. We can control the impact of emotions to some extent by, for example, becoming more analytical and more fact based or by being more aware of the source of the emotion that is guiding us. But we cannot eliminate their influence. Remember, without emotions, we are often unable to make a decision at all. Also, emotions may influence our subconscious more often than they influence our conscious. The good news is that our emotions are designed into the process in a way that helps us get to the right answer effortlessly and efficiently, most of the time. But in the wrong situation, as happened to Wang and General Browning, they can lead us to disaster.

Errors in our thinking that come from misrecognizing a pattern or from a misleading emotional tag are particularly troublesome because we make decisions one plan at a time. As we shall see in the next chapter, our thinking process gives us few opportunities to catch these errors before they have influenced our decision.

FOUR

One Plan at a Time

ADMIRAL YAMAMOTO ISOROKU was commander in chief of Japan's Imperial Combined Fleet. He was a brilliant commander. A charismatic and ambitious man, Yamamoto had risen almost to the top of his profession despite the fact that he had championed some unpopular causes (or maybe because of it). He supported the international naval treaties before the war that kept Japan's fleet smaller than those of the United States and Britain. He also supported the development of naval aviation during a period when battleships were seen as the trump card. He argued against an alliance with Nazi Germany. He was used to taking controversial positions, and he was often proved right.

By 1942, Yamamoto had led the Imperial Combined Fleet for three years. He had built up a staff group of radical thinkers and had been in frequent conflict with Naval General Staff (the officers in charge of all of Japan's naval forces), with Imperial Headquarters (the supreme command of Japan's army, navy, and air force), and with officers reporting to him. Yet his position was unchallenged. He had argued for a decisive blow against the United States at the outset of war and had been credited with the Pearl Harbor success. He had even threatened to resign when his Pearl Harbor campaign was challenged. Naval General Staff had argued that the Americans would be unlikely to go to war unless directly provoked. Admiral Yamamoto dismissed this as wishful thinking and put his career on the line. In the following year, the Imperial Navy swept all before it, routing the British and the Dutch and dominating the South Pacific and parts of the Indian Ocean.

The decision he now faced was what to do next.[1] Yamamoto's plan was to focus on the Central Pacific around Hawaii, with the objective of dealing a further, decisive defeat to the United States Navy. At Pearl Harbor, the Imperial Navy had failed to put the American aircraft carriers out of action. Believing that naval aircraft were likely to be the deciding weapon of this Pacific War, Yamamoto was searching for a strategy that would bring the American carriers into combat before the U.S. Navy was strong enough to win the battle. He therefore proposed invading Hawaii.

The army, whose support would be needed for any option, was over-stretched. Army commanders argued strongly against any increase in territory. They felt they only had sufficient resources for Japan's current gains. Japan controlled a vast area stretching from Manchuria in the north to the Solomon Islands in the south and from Burma in the west to Wake Island in the mid-Pacific. The army's position effectively ruled out an invasion of Hawaii.

But Admiral Yamamoto was not easily distracted from his original idea. He continued to plan a campaign in the Central Pacific. Since Hawaii was out of the question, because of the support he would need from the army, Yamamoto planned to target Midway, a tiny atoll at the western end of the Hawaiian chain of islands, more than 1,000 miles from Oahu. He calculated that the Americans would not relinquish Midway without a major sea battle: it was an important flying boat base from which they patrolled the west Pacific.

A major sea battle would give Japan the opportunity to sink the American carriers and win final control of the Pacific, bringing the Americans to the bargaining table. For Admiral Yamamoto, this was to be the decisive battle. As it turned out, Midway was indeed a decisive battle: it spelled the end of Japan's Pacific successes.

Superior Plans

Yamamoto's plan was strongly criticized by Imperial Headquarters and Naval General Staff. Three objections were made. First, Japan's successes since Pearl Harbor had come from expanding under the cover of land-based air support; the attack on Midway would put the navy at a disadvantage because it would be in range of American land-based air support, but not Japanese land-based support. Second, it would be hard to defend Midway because of the strength of American submarine forces. Third, knowing that they could retake Midway at will, the Americans would not expose themselves to a sea battle unless they were confident of winning.

Naval General Staff concluded that an alternative strategy of cutting supply lines to Australia was clearly superior.

Admiral Yamamoto responded by sending his staff officers to argue with Naval General Staff. He dismissed the Southwest Pacific option, arguing that the best way to cut supply lines was to destroy the navy that protected them. He also pointed out that if the Americans chose not to defend Midway, Japan would win a bloodless victory that would sap U.S. morale and make peace negotiations more likely. Moreover, his dismissive attitude made it clear that he was again prepared to resign if he did not get his way. Under pressure, his superiors backed down, and preparations for an attack on Midway began in earnest.

One of the most fascinating parts of the ensuing month was the war games held on board battleship *Yamato* on May 1–5, 1942. To an objective observer, these exercises demonstrated many of the flaws in the Central Pacific plan.

When the officer playing the red team (American forces) chose tactics that exposed weaknesses in the battle plan, the umpire, Admiral Yamamoto's chief of staff, ruled against them. At one point, the red team followed tactics that were close to those actually used by the Americans during the battle. They arrived at Midway earlier than expected, inflicted crippling damage to the Japanese carriers, and disrupted the landing force. The games umpire ruled that these tactics were impossible, reversed the damage, and insisted that the red team follow a plan closer to the one the Japanese navy was expecting.

At another point, the Japanese fleet was under attack from American land-based aircraft. When the umpire for this engagement rolled the dice to determine the damage, he produced fourteen direct hits, resulting in the loss of two Japanese carriers. Again the games umpire intervened, revising the number of hits down to three.

Despite these and many other warning signs, the plans for the Central Pacific campaign remained largely unchanged. At the end of May, the Japanese fleet left Hashirajima Bay and headed for Midway. On June 14, a shattered fleet returned defeated and depleted. The Imperial Navy had lost its strongest weapon, its carrier division advantage. Before Midway, Japan had a six-to-four advantage in fleet carriers. After the battle, the United States had a three-to-two advantage. In addition, Japan suffered a huge setback in its naval aviation capability: 140 pilots and 720 technicians. Admiral Yamamoto had chosen his strategy with the objective of inflicting this kind of damage on his enemy. Instead, he had inflicted it on his own navy.

So why did Admiral Yamamoto and the staff of the Combined Fleet insist on a strategy that proved to be so flawed, and why were the flaws in this strategy not properly exposed? The answer is the subject of many books and will be debated by historians for years to come. We believe Yamamoto is an example of a third mental habit that increases the likelihood of making flawed decisions: one-plan-at-a-time decision making.

If our brains naturally questioned and challenged our assessments and judgments or normally compared multiple options—as we are advised to do by most decision scientists—we would be much better at spotting errors in our thinking and correcting them. We would be more likely to make the right decisions even when our initial thoughts are influenced by one or more of the red flag conditions.

But we do not. This is not how our brains evolved. Our brains do not have strong processes for questioning our initial assessment of a situation, nor do they naturally juggle multiple options. We have evolved a brain that assesses the situation, comes up with a plan of action, and then evaluates that plan. Only if the evaluation exposes some problem do we then cycle back and look for another plan that avoids the problem.

How We Make Decisions

Gary Klein has been studying decision making for twenty years. He refers to his research as the study of "naturalistic" decision making because he does field research rather than clinical experiments. In his remarkable 1998 book, *Sources of Power*, he notes, "I have slept in fire stations, observed intensive care units, and ridden in M-1 tanks, U.S. Navy AEGIS cruisers, Blackhawk helicopters, and AWACS aircraft."[2]

Klein is a careful researcher, making sure he does not claim more than his research suggests. He believes he understands how "experienced decision makers" cope when faced with "high stakes, inadequate information, ill-defined goals, poorly defined procedures, the need to perceive patterns, rich context of higher-level goals, stress, dynamic conditions, team coordination and time pressure." Moreover, he believes that his findings hold even when time pressure is absent. In other words, the situations he studies are similar to those facing Admiral Yamamoto.

In one of his first studies, Klein worked with firefighters. Early on he was interviewing an experienced fireground commander. He explained his desire to research decision making. The fireman asked him what he meant by a "decision." He responded that a decision involved a choice among options. The fireman retorted that he did not make decisions. Surprised, Klein pointed out that the fireman must frequently be faced with situations where he needed to make a decision about what he or his team should do. Yet the fireground commander continued to argue that he did not make decisions: he did not make a choice between alternatives. When faced with a situation, he did what needed to be done.

It was only after Klein had completed his research that he understood these seemingly contradictory comments. Klein discovered that people with experience do most of their decision making unconsciously.

They assess the situation by drawing on similar experiences from their memory, but much of this assessment process happens unconsciously. They then select a course of action from their memories of past actions. The scanning of these memories also happens unconsciously. Finally, they test the practicality of this course of action by imagining what will happen if the action is taken. This imagining activity is the main conscious work that happens during a decision. What Klein had discovered is that we mostly make decisions unconsciously using experience, intuition, and imagination. We do not normally do much conscious analysis, such as identifying and comparing options or challenging assumptions and initial assessments.

Klein gives an example of a fire reported in the basement of a four-story apartment building. On arrival, the commander sees no smoke or flames. He finds a door to the basement, enters, and sees flames spreading up the laundry chute. He immediately sends firemen up the building to get above the fire and spray water down onto it. Afterward, he was able to explain that he diagnosed a vertical fire spreading straight up, and because there were no signs of smoke, it must have been just starting. Hence his plan to get above the fire before it developed into something more serious. Unfortunately, at each floor, the firemen found the fire had passed them.

When they reported back, the commander walked around to the front of the building to reassess the situation and saw smoke coming out from under the roof. Immediately, he switched to a search-and-rescue strategy, ordered his team to get everyone out of the building, and called for more help. When asked about this decision, he explained that he concluded that the fire must have just hit the top of the chute and was burning the underside of the roof. Since this was a much more dangerous situation, he changed plans.

As Klein notes, "Where were the decisions?" At no point did the commander weigh options. He certainly made decisions. But he did not make choices between alternatives. At each point, he knew what to do. He assessed the situation and decided what to do without any apparent intervening steps.

It turns out that fireground commanders rarely compare alternatives. They only use a process of comparing options when they face "radically unfamiliar situations"—in other words, when they have no relevant experience to draw on. In situations where they feel reasonably competent, they seem to leap straight to an answer. Out of 156 decisions analyzed during his study, the commanders considered options only 18 times. On 138 occasions they simply considered one plan and executed it.

These findings and their consistency across many different situations and organizations are important to decision making. When we feel we have relevant experience, we normally make decisions without much analysis. This is not true for all types of decisions, and it may not be true for all individuals. In some situations, such as buying an appliance or a house, we are confronted with choices in a way that makes it hard to avoid considering options. Some people are naturally more analytical and enjoy laying out the options and considering them. However, as Klein's research has demonstrated in many different environments, the vast majority of the time, we use a one-plan-at-a-time process to make decisions.

Primed to Decide

Klein's conclusion is amply reinforced by our own fieldwork. In over 80 percent of the cases where we had personal contact with the prime decision maker, he or she appeared to have arrived at judgments about the right course of action without careful weighing of the options. It was certainly true of Yamamoto. And as we monitored our own decisions during the research project (how many cases to do, how to represent our model visually, how many chapters to have in the book), we found that we were also following a one-plan-at-a-time process.

Klein labeled this decision-making process the recognition-primed decision (RPD) model, to contrast it with the classical decision models that rely on comparisons between options. Klein used this label because he wanted people to understand that the normal decision process is one that is primed by our subconscious recognition mechanisms and that these influence the rest of the process.

While we agree that the decision process starts with an assessment based on pattern recognition, we feel that the more interesting feature of the process is the fact that our brains naturally assess only one plan of action at a time. We do not naturally lay out options and evaluate alternatives. We rely on our unconscious processes to bring a plan of action into our consciousness, and then assess that plan to see whether it makes sense, before considering others.[3] If we imagine that our first plan will work, we do not normally consider alternatives, or if we do, we give them little attention. We label the model the one-plan-at-a-time process (see figure 4-1). It is broadly the same as Klein's RPD model.

First, we receive some sensory inputs. Our pattern recognition processes then scan our memory for similar past experiences. At the same time, our brain accesses the emotions tagged to those past experiences. This leads to an assessment of the situation, together with an action orientation. For example, the fireground commander assessed the fire as just starting up the laundry chute, which, based on past experience and training, suggested quick but not life-or-death action. Others have referred to this orientation step as "framing the problem."[4] During this first part of the process, we are making an assessment of what is happening and what sort of a response it requires.

Once we have made an assessment, we appear to do some checking of our thinking. We look for what Klein called *cues*: things we would ex-

FIGURE 4-1

The one-plan-at-a-time process

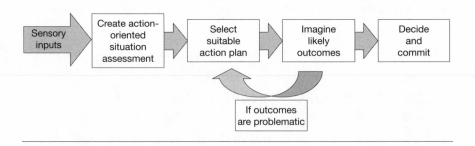

pect to see if our assessment was right. For example, the fireman noted that there was not much smoke, confirming his view that the fire had only just started. What is important here is that we do not actively search for disconfirming information. Also, much of this checking is happening unconsciously. In other words, we are not consciously stopping our thinking and checking our assessment, but our subconscious alerts us if things we would expect to see, given our assessment, are not apparent, or if something unexpected occurs, such as the reports that the fire has gotten above the firemen.

Now that we have an assessment, we start to think of an action plan. But we do this one plan at a time. The fireman's first idea was to get above the flames, and he did not compare this in his mind with alternatives. The first action plan that comes to mind will be one that our subconscious has spotted as a result of scanning memories of similar situations and their emotional tags.

Now that we have a plan, we consciously check it out by imagining what will happen. To do this simulation, we tap into our theories about how things work: the models we have built up from our learning and our experience. We use these to imagine the likely outcomes of the plan, and we then evaluate these outcomes by accessing the emotional tags associated with them. Outcomes with negative emotional tags signal to us that there is a problem.

If we spot a problem, we will cycle back and look for another plan. The process of choosing another plan is the same as before. Our subconscious scans our memories of previous plans and brings one into consciousness that does not have the problems of the first plan, but still has a positive emotional connection to our action orientation. We then repeat the simulation, checking out this new plan by imagining what will happen.

Experts rarely need to consider more than one plan. As with the fireman, their first plan is a good one. When we have a plan that works, we have decided; we do not feel the need to consider other plans, unless, of course, they are presented to us by colleagues. Our last act, as we decide, is to tag that decision with an emotion based on our level of commitment. This tag is probably a function of the confidence we have in the plan based on our imagination of what will happen and the positive emotions we have toward the expected outcomes. (See figure 4-2 for a full layout of the one-plan-at-a-time process.)

So how can the red flag conditions distort our thinking in the one-plan-at-a-time process?

Misleading experiences are most likely to disrupt our thinking in the situation assessment stage, either because we misrecognize the pattern or because the emotion tagged to the pattern gives us an unsuitable action orientation. But misleading experiences can also cause us to select an unsuitable plan and make bad judgments about outcomes. Hence the phrase "Generals are usually fighting the last war."

Misleading prejudgments are most likely to create distortions when we evaluate outcomes: they cause us to get committed to

FIGURE 4-2

The one-plan-at-a-time decision process

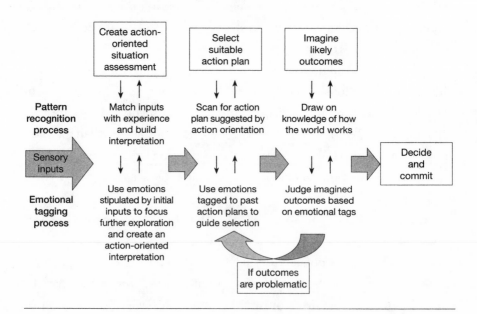

the wrong plans. But they can also cause us to misjudge the situation or to be fixated on a particular plan of action—often something that has worked in the past. Hence the phrase "To a man with a hammer, everything looks like a nail."

Inappropriate self-interest and **inappropriate attachments** are most likely to affect the way we evaluate outcomes: they can cause us to become committed to the wrong plans by giving those plans strong positive tags. But they can also disrupt our thinking earlier in the process. They can steer us toward inappropriate plans because they affect the emotional tags we attached to those plans in the past. They can even affect our situation assessment by causing us to pay too much attention to our personal interests or our attachments. Hence the phrase, "It is hard to get a man to do something, when his salary depends on his not doing it."

The one-plan-at-a-time process involves both pattern recognition and emotional tagging to arrive at both a decision and a level of commitment. Unfortunately, it is a process that is not well designed for challenging and correcting our assessments and judgments. We are only likely to question our starting orientation if important cues are missing or if we find it hard to think of any plan that has positive outcomes. We are only likely to question our initial plan of action if we imagine negative outcomes. Finally, if we misjudge the outcomes, the process has no step that would cause us to revisit these judgments. In other words, the mental process we have is well designed for helping us make quick decisions when we have plenty of relevant experience and our judgments are good, but it is poorly designed for helping us cope with ambiguous situations where we have little prior knowledge of what to do or situations where our memories or emotions may start our thinking down the wrong path.[5]

Admiral Yamamoto's Decision

Let us now try to understand Admiral Yamamoto's decision through the one-plan-at-a-time process.

Creating an Action-Oriented Situation Assessment

Admiral Yamamoto had been receiving inputs about the successes in the Pacific, about the fact that the U.S. aircraft carriers were still a threat, and about the lull in the demands on the Imperial Navy expected in coming months. His assessment was that the Imperial Navy needed to define a new plan, with the prime objective of neutralizing the American navy.

How did Yamamoto reach this assessment? In the same way that the fireground commander assessed the fire as having just started in the laundry chute: by processing the inputs and using experience to develop an interpretation. Much of this processing is unconscious.

Let's unpick Yamamoto's assessment further. One part of his assessment was that the American aircraft carriers were a major continuing threat. He may have focused on this issue because of his training, because he had championed the development of naval air power in the Imperial Navy, or because he had seen the power of his own carriers in the Pacific War. Some combination of these would have given Yamamoto a strong negative emotional tag to "enemy carriers," causing him to have an action orientation of "something needs to be done about them."

Another part of his assessment, a part that was less near the surface but probably underpinning his action orientation, was that further attacks on Americans would be likely to bring them to the bargaining table rather than cause them to dig deeper for a long war. Why did he not realize that the Americans, with or without carriers, were a huge threat? Why did he not focus on the economic muscle the Americans had to reequip faster than Japan and the risk of further antagonizing them? Again, we can explain this in terms of experience. Yamamoto—and in recent history, Japan—had not fought against a stronger economy. Each of its previous wars had been against less developed economies. Hence there were probably no emotional tags alerting him to the importance of America's economic strength.

A third part of Yamamoto's assessment was his orientation toward engineering a major naval engagement. Again, this can be explained through his experience. Admiral Yamamoto had learned his naval skills in the period after the Russo-Japanese War. In 1905, Japan had achieved one of the most decisive naval battles in history at Tsushima. The Japanese sank or captured almost all of the Russian fleet for the loss of a handful of small boats and a hundred or so sailors. The lessons from this success, passed down to younger officers, were the importance of offensive rather than defensive tactics and the need to engineer major sea battles. The Japanese were not alone in this strategic view. It was largely the policy of the British Royal Navy, which had been the world's strongest navy.

The Imperial Navy became further convinced of these policies as its power in the Pacific increased. In the war with China, in the Indian Ocean campaign, and at other battles in the South Pacific, the policy of aggressive naval engagements succeeded. As a result, Yamamoto was likely to have had a positive emotional tag associated with the idea of a major naval engagement.

A fourth part of Yamamoto's assessment was his presumption of success in a major sea battle. This would have been partly a conscious rational calculation: at this point in the war, the Imperial Navy was the stronger force. But it would probably also have been an unconscious emotional judgment. Japan had not lost a naval engagement for years. Yamamoto had never lost a major sea battle. His emotions would have been telling him that he would succeed again.

The net result of these assessments was that Yamamoto saw this situation as an opportunity to draw the U.S. Navy into a decisive battle that would provide a conclusive Japanese victory.

Selecting an Action Plan

Yamamoto then needed a plan, and he concluded that the appropriate action was to bring the U.S. Navy into a major sea battle by invading Hawaii. Why did he focus on this plan?

We do not have evidence that Yamamoto considered a range of plans, although it is likely that his staff must have explored more than just the Hawaii option. Hawaii may have had a strong positive emotional tag in Yamamoto's mind as a result of the Pearl Harbor success. But it may just have been the most obvious way of enticing the Americans to fight. The earlier analysis, and historical accounts, suggest that his focus was on engineering a major sea battle. Hawaii was less important.

Imagining the Likely Outcome

Yamamoto then imagined what would happen if he executed this plan. To do so, he drew on his knowledge of how to fight sea battles, of the fighting skills of his navy, of the relative strengths of the two navies, of the waters they would fight in, and so on. Inevitably, he was influenced by Japan's successes in Russia, in China, at Pearl Harbor, and in the Pacific. He could see no major problems. In fact, the only concern he kept returning to was the fear that the Americans would not fight. Hence, his thinking was focused on how to ensure that the American fleet would come to battle, rather than on whether the Imperial Navy would win the engagement. As a result, Yamamoto decided that the Hawaii plan was a good one, and proposed it to Naval General Staff, his direct superiors.

Interestingly, other plans were circulating in Naval General Staff and Imperial Headquarters at the time. One was to switch from an offensive to a defensive stance. Admiral Kusaka, a member of Naval General Staff, was a leading proponent of this policy. He believed that Japan should consolidate its gains and build strong defenses against an American counterattack. Japan, he believed, could discourage the United States from a long Pacific War, if its resistance was sufficiently strong and it did not threaten additional U.S. territory.

A second option, coming out of staff work at Imperial Headquarters, was aimed at the Indian Ocean. Japan would attack the British in India, stimulating an Indian uprising and opening a land link with its European allies through a Middle East corridor. The Indian campaign surprisingly had some army support, because with an Indian uprising, it would take few troops. It would also open up the possibility of aid from Japan's European allies.

A third option was to cut the line of supply from the United States to Australia and so prevent a buildup of military capability in Australia.

Admiral Inoue, in charge of the Southwest Pacific, was a strong champion for this option. The Americans had, during the spring of 1942, launched two successful and daring raids in his area. Admiral Inoue needed reinforcements. Naval General Staff also believed that this plan was superior to Yamamoto's.

Yamamoto appeared to give little more than a cursory assessment of these alternatives. He continued to push the plan for invading Hawaii, until he was forced to reconsider by the army's refusal to support an invasion of Hawaii. At that point, rather than examining the alternative plans in detail, Yamamoto continued to focus on his idea of a major sea battle. He therefore looped back to the plan selection stage of the one-plan-at-a-time process and concluded that there was another way of bringing the Americans into a major sea battle, one that would not require army support. So he developed a new plan to invade Midway. Once the Hawaii option was ruled out, Yamamoto did not appear to reconsider his initial assessment and orientation toward a major sea battle. Instead, he looked for a way of engineering a major sea battle without involving army support.

Again he would have imagined what would happen and, using a thinking process similar to that of the Hawaiian invasion, concluded that the plan would succeed. He never imagined a defeat. He only imagined the problem of the Americans refusing to fight for Midway. In which case, he envisaged capturing the island without losses and further eroding American morale.

Committing to Action

Yamamoto then started preparing for a battle around Midway and persuading his superiors and colleagues that this was the right plan. In his mind, he would have made the decision, and he would probably have tagged it with a strong positive emotion. This strong commitment and the fact that he was used to pushing decisions through despite opposition would have caused him to brush aside the objections of his superiors. Their concerns were recognized, but would have had weak emotional tags in Yamamoto's mind. He seemed so unimpressed by their arguments that he did not bother to address them himself: he sent one of his staff to argue with his bosses.

Having won the arguments with his own staff, having won the arguments with Naval General Staff, Yamamoto would have added more positive emotional tags to the plan. His commitment would probably have been apparent to his subordinates and contributed to the fiasco of the war games on board battleship *Yamato*.

Unconscious Yamamoto

We believe that leaders, like Admiral Yamamoto, when facing an important decision, use a mainly unconscious process involving pattern recognition and emotional tagging both to assess the situation and to identify a suitable action plan. Whether it is about a battle plan, a building fire, an investment in new technology, or a new appointment, they will then use imagination to test the quality of their plan, and only adjust it if they identify a major flaw in the plan. Once they have a plan that passes their mental simulation, they will believe they have the right answer and may commit to it strongly.

In our work, we observe this behavior frequently. Many leaders form judgments about the situation without fully exploring the range of alternative explanations, and they select action plans without laying out all the options or clarifying the criteria needed to choose between options. Often, it falls to their subordinates to test the plan or carry out more detailed analysis. But because the subordinates know that the leader already has a view, they overlook some options or override the analysis (as in the war games for Midway).

The core message is that our one-plan-at-a-time way of making decisions does not provide us with strong checks and balances against errors in our thinking. It is a highly efficient process when our experience, knowledge, and emotional tags are guiding us to the right answer. But it is not well designed for helping us question and challenge the judgments we make. As a result, when red flag conditions exist, we need to design steps into the process that will provide some safeguard against error. In part 2 we will describe each of the red flags in more detail. In part 3 we will discuss safeguards and how to choose effective ones.

PART TWO

Why Decisions Go Wrong

FIVE

Misleading Experiences

I N THE 1980S AND 1990S, Sir Clive Thompson was chief executive of one of the most successful companies in Europe: Rentokil. Thompson was lauded—nominated as the best CEO in Britain on more than one occasion—and Rentokil had been voted the United Kingdom's best-run company.

Thompson created a uniquely disciplined, yet entrepreneurial culture at Rentokil and focused on markets, such as pest control and office plants, where there were opportunities to earn exceptional margins. He became known as Mr. 20 Percent: the man who succeeded in delivering annual profit increases of 20 percent every year.

By the early 1990s, Thompson had been in charge of Rentokil for more than ten years. Growth had come from a relentless combination of margin improvement, market share gains, and small add-on acquisitions. He was operating in fragmented markets where most competitors were small and many were for sale. In ten years, the company had made 130 acquisitions.

Then, under pressure to continue the company's growth trajectory, he started looking for larger deals. Add-on acquisitions simply could not deliver the 20 percent increases of previous years. He acquired Securi-guard in 1994, increasing the size of Rentokil by 30 percent, and followed it by acquiring BET in 1996, more than doubling the company's size again. The BET deal led to a new name, Rentokil Initial.

Unfortunately, the large deals proved unsuccessful. Mr. 20 Percent tumbled off his perch. Shares halved in value and then halved again. Thompson tried to recover by selling some of the things he had bought and going back to basics. Too late. The culture he had so carefully created was undermined and diluted. It proved impossible to go back. He tried passing the baton and taking a lesser role as chairman. In the end Thompson was asked to step out of a board meeting so that the directors could discuss his position. When he returned, he was asked to resign.

What caused Thompson to change a successful strategy? What was he thinking? He was well advised. He would have been told that there were risks. He would have had tough questions from his shareholders. In fact, during the acquisition battle, the management team of BET produced a well-argued defense document pointing out most of the risks that subsequently proved to be real. Why wasn't Thompson able to see the risks he was taking with everything he had created?

Driven by Experience

This example, as with many of our flawed strategy cases, has multiple potential explanations. Thompson could have made a prejudgment that the 20 percent target was vital and that he needed to take high risks to achieve it. Thompson could also have been influenced by self-interest. Maybe his stock options were structured to encourage him to take too much risk. However, the explanation that seems to fit best with Thompson's own reflections is that he was misled by his experience: his pattern recognition caused him to see big acquisitions as being similar to the many small successful acquisitions he had made over the last ten years. Instead of fish and fowl, he saw simply larger fish. Also he had strong positive emotions about doing deals and taking acquisition-oriented risks.

When Thompson talked to classrooms of managers at the time of the BET deal and soon after, he was often confronted with some skepticism. Students were concerned that he was taking too much risk.

In response, he explained that Rentokil had made more than 100 acquisitions and that he needed to provide additional deals to keep his aggressive management team in work: "I need to give my lions more red
meat," he said.[1] He would also share some of his thinking about the
risks and benefits, concluding that the risks were worth taking. But, to
the listener, the explanation felt partial or insufficient, and Thompson
felt only partly engaged in the question. He seemed to be making his
judgment through some process other than a careful assessment of the
risks and benefits. He appeared to be comparing the big acquisitions
with the previous 130 deals and concluding that success was likely.

But it was not a case purely of flawed pattern recognition. Thompson
was also drawing on some strong emotional connections. He came alive
when he switched to telling stories. One story was about risk. Thompson had been given shares in two companies during his teens. One of
them, Slater Walker, was the darling of the market. The company acquired businesses and improved them, like today's private equity funds.
Its shares rose fast. Then the company collapsed, and Thompson lost all
his money.

The other company, Trust House Forte, was an ambitious hotel company. The founder, Charles Forte, made a number of bold acquisitions
of hotel and catering businesses and succeeded. The stock quadrupled
in value. Thompson said this experience stimulated his interest in acquisitions and in risk.

He also liked to tell assembled groups about the excitement of the
deal process: the early morning meetings; the discussions about bid
tactics with investment bankers; the dangers of letting bankers take too
much control; the development of arguments for the bid documents;
the knowledge that the defending company was going through the same
processes at the same moment but probably with less experience.

He also recalled the excitement of waiting for the result of the shareholder votes. In the BET case, Rentokil won the day minutes before the
deadline, when an aging clerk hobbled into the counting office and handed
over a large bundle of votes in Rentokil's favor. Those votes tipped
the balance. It was a very close-run fight. Thompson was standing by

the counting desk, watching the clerk arrive. He liked to speculate about what might have happened to him personally if this clerk had lost his way or been taken ill. The votes would have missed the deadline, and, as Thompson liked to speculate, the Rentokil board would probably have asked him to resign.

At the end of these stories, with eyes alight, Thompson would comment, "Better to live like a lion for a day than a lifetime as a lamb." In other words, Thompson was motivated by strong positive feelings about risk, the excitement of the chase and the thrill of winning. His previous experiences had given him emotional tags that may have contributed to misleading him over these big acquisition deals. He knew he was taking a significant risk, but because of his previous experience with acquisitions, he probably underestimated the risk, and because of his strong positive emotions for doing deals, he readily concluded that the risks were worth taking.

Unconsciously Misled

Rentokil provides an illustration of our first red flag condition: misleading experiences. When our memory contains an experience that has some similarities to the situation, but also some important differences, we can be misled into forming a view of the situation or choosing a course of action that is misguided. For example, none of Thompson's previous acquisitions were public companies of the size of Securiguard or BET. We make these kinds of errors quite frequently, and most of the time we catch the error as we look more closely at the situation, imagine how our actions will play out, or get additional information. However, particularly when we have been very successful in the past, as Thompson had been, we can often presume that our actions will be successful, and we will find it hard to question ourselves and correct our error.

So how do we know that Sir Clive Thompson was influenced by misleading experiences? We don't. In fact, the tricky part is that Thompson would not know either. These processes are unconscious. Moreover, the rational part of our brain is so inventive that it will, if challenged, produce a rational explanation for a decision that has been made intu-itively. It may not be an explanation that will convince an objective lis-tener. But it will convince the person giving the explanation. In other words, the person whose decision is influenced by pattern recognition and emotional tags will not believe that it was.

Misleading experience is a common contributory factor to flawed de-cisions. In our database, it was a major or contributory factor in almost two-thirds of the cases. Matthew Broderick's response to Katrina was influenced by his experiences with hurricanes that had struck land that was above rather than below sea level. An Wang had positive experiences taking on IBM by launching a proprietary word processor—but failed when he applied the same formula to the personal computer. Admiral Yamamoto's decision to draw out and attack the U.S. Navy at Midway was shaped by his personal experiences, and those of the Japanese navy, in crushing the Russian and Chinese navies using just such tactics. Quaker's chairman mistook Snapple for an opportunity that was similar to Gatorade only to find out that Snapple's weak position, unique rela-tionship with its distributors, and unusual culture made it a very differ-ent animal.

Misleading experiences will not always unbalance the decision maker. If the decision maker has sufficient relevant experience, he or she will not need to draw on misleading experiences or will be able to correct the initial mistake. Gatorade and Snapple may have looked similar, but someone who had worked in the type of entrepreneurial, quirky envi-ronment that characterized Snapple would have quickly sensed the dif-ference between the companies. While Quaker management's instinct was to "Gatorize" Snapple, someone with more relevant experience would have seen the difficulties in integrating the two companies. They might have kept Snapple separate initially, to sort out the operational problems before integrating the businesses on a more selective basis. Past experiences are only likely to be misleading to the decision maker who has insufficient relevant experience. A lack of sufficient relevant experience is, therefore, a precondition that opens the door to mislead-ing experiences.

Risky Shortcuts

Two effects that are well supported in clinical studies provide evidence for our proposition that decision makers are often misled by their experiences.

The first effect is known as the *availability heuristic.*[2] A heuristic is an approach or shortcut that the brain takes to solve a problem. According to the availability heuristic, we judge the frequency, probability, or likely causes of an event by the degree to which instances or occurrences of that event are readily "available" in memory, rather than by a careful assessment of all the data. A memory may be available because it evokes an emotion, is vivid, is easily imagined, or is specific (rather than unemotional, bland, difficult to imagine, or vague). The availability heuristic is mainly about emotional tagging. Vivid, emotional, or easily imagined events are likely to be tagged with an emotion and, as a result, are more likely to be brought into focus by our brains than equally relevant events that have neutral emotional tags.

In one lab study, people are read lists of names of well-known personalities of both genders. Different lists are presented to two groups. In one list the women's names are relatively more famous than the men's, but the list contains more men than women. In the other list the situation is reversed. More women's names, but the men's are more famous.

After hearing the list of names, participants in both groups are asked to decide whether the list contains more men or women. Both groups get the answer wrong. Both guess the gender that has the more famous rather than the more numerous names.[3] The explanation is that the more famous names are more available in the memory, so it appears to the listener that the list has more names of that gender. In our terminology, the more famous names would have had stronger emotional tags; hence they would have demanded more attention in the one-plan-at-a-time decision process.

The availability heuristic not only reinforces the proposition that we use emotional tags to focus our thinking during the one-plan-at-a-time decision process—it also demonstrates the potential that exists for the process to mislead us. Personal experiences are going to be more vivid and more specific than stories we have been told or material we have been taught. Experiences with strong emotions are more available than those with neutral emotions. In other words, our minds can link with an experience for reasons other than its relevance to the situation we are considering. Obviously, the experience needs to be similar to the situation. But the availability heuristic reminds us that an experience can influence our thinking more than it should because of its availability.

In the Rentokil story, there is an example of this availability point. A few months before Rentokil's bid for BET, Granada, a catering and media conglomerate, bid for Trust House Forte, the company Thompson had invested in when he was a teenager. It was a high-profile hostile deal, the first big hostile deal in the London stock market for five years. Moreover, Trust House Forte was a bigger company than Granada. The management team leading the deal, Gerry Robinson and Charles Allen, were much praised for their boldness. The different nature of the businesses and the risks of overdiversification did not seem to be a major concern to shareholders or the financial press. Robinson and Allen were seen as being supercapable managers able to apply their magic to this new area. Not surprisingly, this deal was prominent in Thompson's mind. He would refer to it when explaining his own deal. Clearly, it had some relevance to Thompson's decision, but its availability may have caused it to have more influence on Thompson than its relevance warranted.

The availability heuristic has a number of associated subeffects. The *recency and vividness bias* claims that we access recent and vivid information more than older and less vivid information, even if the latter is more relevant. The *retrievability bias* claims that we make more use of easy-to-access information and memories, even when harder-to-access information is more relevant. The *presumed association bias* claims that when we are asked whether there is an association between two things, we look for situations where there is an association more than we look for situations where there is no association. As a result, we can overestimate how associated the two things are.[4]

In each of these subeffects, we can see our pattern recognition, emotional tagging, and one-plan-at-a-time processes at work. Since emotional tags fade over time, more recent and more vivid memories are likely to have stronger emotional markers and influence our decisions more than older, less vivid memories (the vividness bias). Since our one-plan-at-a-time decision process is not analytical or thorough in the conventional sense, it is not surprising that we focus more attention on the easy-to-retrieve memories than those buried in our minds (the retrievability bias). Since our pattern recognition process works by looking for a memory that will help with our judgments, it is not surprising that we look for associations when asked whether two things are associated (presumed association bias).

False Analogies

The second effect is called the *representativeness heuristic*. Whereas the availability heuristic describes the way we access memories, the representativeness heuristic describes the way we reason. When confronted with a decision, we tend to look for aspects of the decision that are similar to previous decisions we have made. We then use the simplifying algorithm or analogy that worked for past decisions. However, the algorithm or analogy we use may be inappropriate for the new situation. For example, we will predict the performance of a person based on the way we have categorized people in the past and which category we think this person falls into. We will predict the success of a new product based on the similarity of this product to past successful or unsuccessful product types.[5] To predict the success of Snapple or the BET acquisition, we will look at the success of Gatorade or at other acquisitions we have executed.

The representativeness heuristic leads to a number of biases. One example is the *base rate bias*, in which people make a decision on the basis of only some of the information available to them, and ignore the background ("base rate") information that is implied by the situation but not brought to the fore. An example is when entrepreneurs fail to consider the fact that most ventures fail. They make their judgments about the likelihood of success on the information they have about the venture, and fail to consider the background fact that most ventures fail. As a result, they become too optimistic.

Another bias that results from the representativeness heuristic is the *regression to the mean bias*. If people are asked to estimate the future performance of a business, they will tend to estimate this on the basis of past performance. If the business is performing well, they will assume that it will continue to perform well. They ignore the background information that no business performs well forever.

As with the availability heuristic, experience is the key to avoiding these pitfalls. People who have experienced a venture that fails will be more aware of the risks. If we have experienced a similar situation or if we have relevant experience to draw on, we are much less likely to be affected by these biases.[6]

Identifying Misleading Experiences

The concept of misleading experience is only useful if we can spot it in advance. We need to be able to analyze a specific decision together with the decision makers involved and decide whether a misleading experience is likely to unbalance the decision or not. If we can do this, if we can spot a misleading experience in advance, we are then in a position to strengthen the decision process to reduce the likelihood of making a bad decision. So how do we know when an experience is misleading?

As we have pointed out, if the decision maker has plenty of relevant experience, he or she will normally be able to correct any conscious or unconscious misleading thoughts. Hence the first signal that misleading experiences might be a problem is when the decision maker does not have sufficient *relevant* experience for the decision that is being made. If Sir Clive Thompson had previously made large acquisitions of companies with different cultures and with significant businesses in unfamiliar industries, the risks he was taking would have been much more prominent in his mind. If William Smithburg had previously acquired a struggling drinks brand and integrated it with a different drinks business, then he might have been better able to identify and evaluate some of the challenges involved in acquiring Snapple. Sufficient relevant experience is, therefore, the best defense against breakdowns in our pattern recognition and emotional tagging processes.

But how do we know when a decision maker has sufficient relevant experience? After all, Thompson had made 130 acquisitions. Quaker had similarly acquired and grown a range of consumer product businesses. The answer is to focus on the uncertainties involved in the specific decision at hand. Without uncertainties, a decision is purely a calculation and can be resolved without judgment. It is the existence of uncertainties that requires us to make judgments and hence to draw on pattern recognition and emotional tagging.

In the Rentokil case, Thompson was exposed to a number of uncertainties for which he had little experience. For example, he was bidding for a public company for the first time. How high would he need to bid in order to win the target? He was also acquiring a number of businesses about which his managers had little experience. He had not done this before. Would his well-honed management approach be able to achieve margin growth in these rather different businesses? Finally, in the case of BET, he acquired a company bigger than Rentokil with a very different culture. Would his management team be able to blend the two organizations without losing the magic of the Rentokil culture? For each of these tough-to-answer questions, Thompson did not have enough relevant experience.

Importantly, the lack of relevant experience is not in itself a red flag. Decision makers who recognize they are doing something unfamiliar will normally be cautious and put in place an appropriate decision process. They will seek experts, involve other managers, and increase the amount of analysis. The problem with a lack of relevant experience is that it opens the door to misleading experiences.

As a result, once you are concerned that the decision maker does not have enough relevant experience for the uncertainties involved in the decision, you should look out for experiences that might cause the decision maker to make an incorrect judgment.

To identify these experiences, it can be helpful to look out for three common sources of misleading experience that are present in over 75 percent of our database of decision errors caused primarily by misleading experiences. The three common sources are as follows:

- The organization or the individuals have had an established strategy (that relates to this decision) for a number of years.

- The organization or the individuals have had some particularly successful or unsuccessful experiences in the recent past (that relate to this decision).

- There is an established industry strategy, some important received wisdom, or a recent important event (that relates to this decision).

For example, in the Rentokil case, Thompson had aimed for a 20 percent growth rate each year for more than ten years, fueled by acquisitions (established strategy). Recent successes included successful acquisitions and another year of achieving the 20 percent growth rate (successful experiences). The successful Granada acquisition of Trust House Forte was a vivid event in Thompson's mind (important event). All three common sources of misleading experience were present.[7]

The list of potentially misleading experiences can be long. So it is helpful to focus the analysis on those experiences that might distort the judgment of the decision maker. For example, the established strategy of a 20 percent annual growth rate, fueled by acquisitions, may have caused Thompson to believe that further acquisitions were the best option for Rentokil to pursue. This would have been reinforced by his experiences of Rentokil's track record of successful acquisitions, and Granada's successful acquisition of Trust House Forte.

In the case of Thompson, all of his misleading experiences were biasing his judgment in one way: toward acquisition. In other cases, we may find a more diverse mix of misleading experiences—some resulting in a bias toward one option, others creating a bias toward another choice.

Leading Questions

We have carefully gone over how to identify misleading experiences because to reduce their impact on the decision, we have to be able to diagnose them in advance. The approach to doing so can be summarized through the following three questions:

1. What are the main uncertainties involved in this decision?

2. Do the main decision makers have sufficient relevant experience to be experts at judging these uncertainties?

3. If the answer is no to question 2, do the main decision makers have any experiences that may potentially mislead their judgments with regard to any unfamiliar uncertainties?

These questions can help us identify experiences that might mislead the decision makers and bias their thinking.

Misleading experiences are a common contributor to flawed decisions. Our research suggests that misleading experiences are a significant cause of bad decisions more than half of the time. While on the one hand we should not be surprised by this, given how extensive the scientific evidence is—Gary Klein's fieldwork and the vast body of literature from clinical studies—we cannot help but be struck by how vulnerable we remain.

For organizational leaders, the message is clear. Misleading experiences can disrupt decisions, and hence represent a key red flag that calls out for attention. The good news is that it is very often possible to identify when we are most vulnerable, when we are most likely to believe we are right when really we are wrong.

It should be clear that if you don't have appropriate relevant experience, you are highly likely to use some less relevant experience to help you think through an important uncertainty that must be resolved to make the decision. And when you do so, there is a significant probability that you will be misled by these less relevant experiences. By identifying these experiences, and particularly the ones that might influence your choice, you can identify the particular experiences that are the most worrying red flags. You can then turn your attention to strengthening the decision process in a way that will counterbalance this potentially distorting influence.

Misleading Prejudgments

S TEVE RUSSELL WAS joint managing director of Boots, Britain's largest drugstore chain, between 1997 and 2000, and CEO between 2000 and 2004. We spoke to him in 2006, more than a year after he had resigned following a turbulent time as leader of the company. For years, "Boots the Chemist" was a household name, boasting dominant market share, high margins, and prime retail sites on every British high street. But the company's dominant position left it little opportunity for further growth, and, more worrying, supermarket chains were expanding their range of drugstore products and taking market share.

When Russell became joint managing director, Boots had already tried a number of different ways of growing. One strategy had been to acquire other British retail businesses with growth potential. Another strategy was to take the drugstore business to other countries. The first had been unsuccessful: the new acquisitions had underperformed and were subsequently sold. The second strategy was not showing much promise.

"For at least 10 years I had believed that Boots ought to be able to go from being a pharmacist into health care," explained Russell. "I could see Boots becoming the health care provider to the nation. All my research told me that there was a huge latent desire for additional health provision in Britain. I had been formulating this ambition for Boots since I was merchandising director of Boots the Chemist in the late 1980s. So, when I became CEO, I was determined to make it happen."[1]

Russell's plan was to build on Boots' health and beauty positioning. He discontinued some unrelated lines, expanded the health range, and launched additional health and well-being services, such as dentistry, chiropody, and travel inoculations. Some of these services could be colocated in the retail outlets to utilize spare retail space.

There was broad support for the focus on health and beauty, but some opposition to the move into services. Some board members were lukewarm, and the financial community, in both London and New York, was dubious. "In London, they argued that we should focus on the core. In New York, they were more excited about the growth potential but concerned about the risks," Russell explained.

"These influences did not cause me to be more cautious. I knew that I could not sit around being cautious. If I was going to try to make change of this kind in a public company I needed to push on. I thought it was my role to move Boots forward. Frankly, if people wanted something else, they would need to do it without me. I would not have managed Boots for cash. Even if the logic for focusing on cash had been overwhelming, I still would not have done it. My concern was that the company was on the verge of becoming bereft of hope or ambition."

Unfortunately for Boots and for Russell, although the health and beauty positioning was sound, the strategy of expanding into services did not succeed. With hindsight, Russell commented, "The problem was an execution problem. We did not have the know-how to make these services work. We should not have tried to do so much of it ourselves." Other managers suggested, however, that many of the services Boots tried to enter were inherently low-margin businesses.

Why was Steve Russell so enthusiastic about a services strategy? Why was he comfortable "pushing on" in the face of skepticism? Why did he fail to anticipate the execution challenges that undermined success? The answer lies, at least in part, in the prejudgments he had made ten years earlier, when he was merchandising director of the chain. He decided that Boots could build on and strengthen its retail position by becoming a "health care provider to the nation," and this vision included expanding into health and well-being services.

Tags That Lead Us Astray

Prejudgments influence decisions because of the way we tag our thoughts with emotions. In decision making, it is these emotional tags that help us sort through the many possible interpretations we could make of any situation and the many possible courses of action we could take. Emotional tags speed our pattern recognition and judgment processes.

When we are faced with a situation that looks familiar, we will access our previous knowledge of that situation. If we have previously made judgments about the situation or about what is appropriate action in this situation, these judgments will take prime place in our thinking. Moreover, the stronger the emotions tagged to these judgments, the more they will influence our thinking. If we are concerned about growth because of threats from competitors, as Russell was, and we have a strong emotional tag that the company needs to continue to grow in size and scope, we are likely to view the situation as one in which the choice is between alternative growth strategies. We are unlikely to be able to rethink the problem from a different perspective—such as a choice between different ways to grow the value of the company—which would include considering sale, spin-offs, or refocusing on the core. If someone suggests that we should consider restructuring our core business, we are likely to experience a strong, negative feeling, which stimulates our neocortex to generate arguments against this proposal.

Even if we know that there are some important differences between the situation we face today and the situation under which our previous judgment was made, we may still make a connection to this prejudgment because of the similarities. Despite a desire to be objective and analytical, we can be unable to prevent the emotional tag associated with our prejudgment "Growth is good" influencing our decision.

Strongly tagged prejudgments will influence our decisions because they will attract attention as we consider related problems and opportunities. If the new situation is different, these prejudgments can inappropriately anchor our thinking, disrupt our objectivity, and make it hard for us to think things through afresh when the circumstances change.[2]

We can see this process working in everyday matters. If a person has made a judgment that "I am afraid of dogs," he will feel fear and back away from a dog, even if the dog is known to be harmless. The wife of one of the authors had the frightening experience of a dog jumping up and licking her when she was little. To this day, although she likes the idea of owning a dog, she recoils anytime a dog approaches. The emotional tags connected with these prejudgments are powerful and can override reason.

Russell's decision is a classic example of the influence of prejudgments. This is not to suggest that he carried out no analysis or ignored other options. Russell hired consultants. He involved his managers in developing the thinking. He was supported by an analytically oriented head of strategy. Nevertheless, his preferences were based on his prejudgments, well articulated by his comment "I thought it was my role to move Boots forward. Frankly, if people wanted something else, they would need to do it without me." These prejudgments are likely to have influenced the decisions that were made.

Hoover's Great Depression

Consider another example—this time from the world of government. In the spring of 1930, the Federal Reserve Board and President Herbert Hoover faced an economy in severe decline. The economy had turned down in the spring of 1929. It had been given a further downward push by the Wall Street crash in the autumn of 1929, and by the spring of 1930 was beginning a downward spiral of bankruptcies, bank failures, and retrenchments. So what did the administration do? Hoover cut government spending and increased taxes. A policy more likely to drive the country into the Great Depression could hardly have been conceived even if that had been the policy maker's intention.

We now know, with hindsight, that the intelligent strategy would have been for the government to have increased spending and reduced taxes. What is remarkable, however, is that precisely this thinking was close to the surface. In a series of conferences with business leaders following the Wall Street crash, President Hoover encouraged them to continue making capital investments and to maintain wages. He even initially made a perfunctory tax cut himself. But prejudgments about the importance of a strong currency and a balanced budget prevented him from taking his own advice when applied to government policy.

John Kenneth Galbraith, the Canadian-born Harvard economist and prolific author, has written one of the definitive analyses of the time. He commented, "The balanced budget was not a subject of thought . . . For centuries avoidance of borrowing had protected people from slovenly or reckless public housekeeping . . . Experience had shown that, however convenient [the reasons for a deficit], discomfort or disaster followed in the long run. Those simple precepts of a simple world did not hold amid the growing complexities of the early thirties. Mass unemployment in particular had altered the rules. Events had played a very bad trick on people, but almost no one tried to think out the problem anew."[3]

The commitment to a balanced budget was so deep set that, even in the midst of the appalling suffering of the Great Depression, the Democratic party—the one party that might have thought its way out of the box for humanitarian reasons—in 1932 called for "an immediate and drastic reduction of governmental expenditures" with the objective of achieving at least a 25 percent decrease in the cost of government.

Hoover, and those around him, suffered from a prejudgment that sound economic policy required a balanced budget. Faced with a financial crisis, Hoover would have been unable, as Galbraith describes, to "think out the problem anew." Proposals to stimulate the economy—such as he advised businesses to do, by encouraging them to continue to make capital expenditures and maintain wages—might have seemed attractive until they were associated with the need to run a government deficit, at which point they would have been rejected by the prejudgment "Deficits are bad."

Stuck on Spirits

To further illustrate the power of prejudgments, consider how they affected the decisions of Alfred Russel Wallace. By any standards, Wallace was one of the smartest people and greatest scientists of his time. Independently, Wallace reached the same conclusions as Charles Darwin regarding evolution and natural selection, and their papers were read together before the Linnaean Society in 1858. Wallace also made other important contributions to anthropology and biology in a lengthy and distinguished scientific career.

When he returned from a long period in the East Indies in the 1870s, Wallace became a firm supporter of the highly popular phenomena of mediums and spiritualism. He reported that he had witnessed the materialization of a six-foot sunflower during a séance. As odd as his enthusiasm for spiritualism may be, it was not so surprising for that period when an array of mediums were reported to be performing remarkable feats of writing on slates, raising voices from the dead, and materializing people and objects.

What is particularly interesting about Wallace's enthusiasm for spiritualism is his reaction to the work of a fellow scientist, S. J. Davey. Davey challenged the general belief in mediums, exposing them as frauds. Davey started out as a believer, convinced that he had seen a vision of a friend who had recently died. This led him to attend some séances with William Eglinton, one of the most famous spiritualists of the time. Davey wrote glowing reports about the work of Eglinton and began to believe that he, himself, had mediumistic powers. In one of his own séances, Davey placed some slates on the table and "in the course of a few minutes I lifted up the slates and found the word 'beware' written in large characters across the under side of the slate."[4] Beware, indeed. Davey later learned that his own experiences were hoaxes played on him by his friends. They had written the word *beware* on his slates in part because they had seen Eglinton cheating and wanted Davey to realize his folly.

Davey, then, set out to see whether he could repeat the results of Eglinton and others using trickery. His results are the first systematic

investigation of the fallacies of eyewitness testimony, and are still referred to today because of their careful reporting and exhaustive docu-
mentation. Davey's work demonstrated that eyewitness testimony
about the "achievements" of mediums could not be relied on, and that
their performances could all be achieved by trickery.

Returning to Wallace, none of this moved the great man to question
his original judgment about spiritualism. He wrote to the journal where
Davey's results were published, complaining that Davey had not explained all of his tricks and suggesting that Davey "was really a medium
as well as a conjurer, and that in imputing all his performances to 'trick'
he was deceiving . . . the public." Even after Davey had explained all his
tricks, Wallace continued to energetically challenge all those who suggested that mediums were not what they appeared.[5]

This story is remarkable for shining a light on how even the most rational (Wallace was a scientist) and successful (he was among the most
famous of scientists) among us can be heavily influenced by our prejudgments. We are all vulnerable to becoming anchored by the prior
judgments we have made. Whether we do become anchored or not depends on the strength of the emotional tag we have given the previous
judgment, the degree to which our mind presumes similarity of the current situation with the past situation, and whether we have any counter
experiences or prejudgments. Wallace clearly became anchored to his
belief in the substance of spiritualism. Davey, on the other hand, did
not. On the contrary, Davey had a sufficiently vivid experience (the
tricks played on him by his friends) to cause him to question his previous belief in séances. The embarrassment Davey felt when his friends
exposed their tricks may have been strong enough for him to challenge
the emotions tagged to his previous judgment. For Wallace, the article
written by Davey was probably not an emotional enough experience to
offset the strong emotions tagged to his prejudgment.

To guard against the biasing effects of prejudgments on strategic decisions, we have to be able to identify them in advance of a decision.
And we have to understand which prejudgments are likely to contribute
to a flawed decision and which are not. Before turning to the topic of

how to do this, let's review some of the research that suggests prejudgments contribute to flawed decisions.

Cognitive Dissonance

Leon Festinger, a psychologist who had studied members of a doomsday cult, proposed, as far back as 1956, the theory of cognitive dissonance.[6] He noted our habit of seeking confirming evidence and of inventing sometimes farcical explanations to interpret information that conflicts with our beliefs. When the world did not end at the hands of aliens as predicted, Festinger's cult members concluded that the aliens had changed their minds and saved the world for some special purpose. In other words, they invented an explanation that fit with their original judgment that aliens were in control of the future of the world.

Cognitive dissonance is the incompatibility of two pieces of knowledge. The theory of cognitive dissonance is that we work hard to avoid dissonance in our minds so that if our behaviors are different from our beliefs, we change one or the other. If we have two dissonant facts, we invent an explanation that accepts both or undermines the substance of one or the other. When we hold a strong belief, we readily acknowledge information that supports it and appear to reject or ignore information that contradicts it. In other words, we become easily anchored by a previous belief or prejudgment. Steve Russell, President Hoover, and Alfred Russel Wallace are all examples of this. They all had long-held beliefs that made it very difficult for them to see the situation afresh.

Cognitive dissonance can also influence decisions as they are happening. For example, Admiral Yamamoto (described in chapter 4) selected the Midway strategy because of misleading experiences in previous wars with Russia and China and because of prejudgments about good naval strategy. But having chosen the Midway strategy, Yamamoto then appeared to become anchored to it.

The reports of the war games prior to the battle of Midway make the point. Despite clear evidence from the war games that the Imperial Navy was taking too much risk, Admiral Yamamoto did not reconsider his plan or even make any significant changes to contingency plans. The behavior of the referees during the war games is a classic illustration of cognitive dissonance. When the red team, representing the Americans, arrived at the battle unexpectedly early, the referee declared it impossible and insisted that the red team revert to a strategy more in line with that expected by the Japanese higher command. When the dice were rolled to assess damage during an American bombing raid, they achieved fourteen direct hits and the loss of two Japanese carriers. Again this was dissonant with expectations, and the referee ordered the carriers to be reinstated and the number of direct hits to be reduced to three.

General Browning suffered from the same inability to challenge his prejudgment that Market Garden was a good plan, when confronted with the information about panzer tanks near Arnhem. Instead, he concluded that the officer giving him the information was suffering from stress and could not be relied on.

Getting Anchored

Decision theorists have demonstrated the way human brains become committed to thoughts, facts, and ideas that are already in the brain. A common term for this effect is the *anchoring and adjustment heuristic*.[7] We appear to make assessments by starting from an initial value and adjusting to yield a final judgment. But we do not adjust enough. We are anchored by the starting point.

This effect has been recorded in a variety of different contexts. For example, if you ask someone to write down their Social Security number and then to estimate the population of Southeast Asia or the distance to Mars, their answer will be influenced by the number they wrote down.[8] A similar effect has been observed in negotiations about price. The outcome of the negotiation is significantly affected by the first figure that is mentioned by either party.

Probably the most famous research on anchoring and adjustment, however, was done by Amos Tversky and Daniel Kahneman—Kahneman

was awarded the 2002 Nobel Prize in Economics.[9] They asked participants to estimate the percentage of African countries in the United Nations (UN). Before the participant answered, they spun a specially
numbered wheel of fortune, observed by the participant, and announced the number the wheel stopped at. The result was dramatic.
The number from the wheel of fortune significantly influenced the estimates that participants made. Participants whose wheel number was
ten guessed, on average, twenty-five countries, and participants whose
wheel number was sixty-five guessed, on average, forty-five countries.

The wheel number seems totally unrelated to the question the participants were asked. So why did the brain become anchored to it? Brain scientists have not yet fully explained this. So our explanation is inevitably
speculative. We believe that in the brain the number is associated with the
context in which it arose. The context was the question about the percentage of African countries in the UN. So it would not be surprising for
the brain to scan numbers associated with this context, when seeking
an answer to the question. Unless the brain finds another number related to this context that has a stronger emotional tag, the number from
the wheel of fortune is likely to become the starting point for making an
estimate. If we can be anchored by a number from a wheel that we have
observed spinning, we can certainly be anchored by a prejudgment we
have made, especially if that prejudgment has strong emotional tags.

The particular danger of anchoring and adjustment is that we can
easily think that we have taken account of its effects, when we have
not. People asked to estimate the percentage of African countries in
the UN, and who started with the number ten *did* adjust upward—but
only to an average of twenty-five. Similarly, those who started with the
number sixty-five adjusted downward—but only to forty-five.

Researchers have shown that anchoring also has the effect of making
us selective about information. We search for information that supports
the anchored position and reject other information.[10] This links back to
cognitive dissonance. When we have made a prejudgment, we tend to access information that supports that judgment and reject other information. This explains the seemingly nonsensical way in which smart

people, like Alfred Russel Wallace, can resist evidence that is contrary to what they believe in or why Boots' Steve Russell failed to question his commitment to the services strategy before it was too late.

Overconfidence Bias

Connected to anchoring is the *overconfidence bias*.[11] When we are dealing with unfamiliar issues, we are often overconfident in the judgments we make. In research experiments, participants are typically asked to estimate the distance to the moon or the revenues of Wal-Mart in 2005, or some other obscure fact. Participants are then asked to rate how confident they were in their estimate, usually by asking them to define a range around their initial estimate in which they are confident that the right answer lies. Nearly 50 percent of the time, the right answer is actually outside the range.

Andrew Campbell had personal experience of this phenomenon as a young consultant at McKinsey & Company. He was asked to review presentations to clients that were at least three years old and that involved making some type of forecast. In each instance, the forecasts had been made cautiously by identifying a range of possible outcomes. When Campbell checked the estimates against what had subsequently transpired, he found that in nearly every case, the actual outcome had been outside the range presented.

The explanation for the overconfidence bias is the same as the explanation for the failure to adjust sufficiently from a starting point: anchoring. Once you have made an estimate, you may be anchored by that estimate, causing you to define a range on either side of the estimate that is too narrow. We can also explain this in terms of neurons and prejudgments. Once you have made a judgment, you have rearranged some neurons and created some emotional tags. That rearrangement and tagging is likely to influence your next judgment on a similar topic. Steve Russell had made judgments about the attractiveness of the health-care sector for Boots, and he became overconfident in these judgments as regards the services element of the strategy. Moreover, his overcommitment was evident to others. He explained that as performance started to slip, some of his subordinates disguised the bad news because they knew he was committed to this strategy.

Interestingly, the overconfidence bias disappears when we are dealing with familiar issues, an outcome we would expect given our understanding of how the brain works. Faced with a problem, the brain searches for useful experiences and prejudgments that connect to the problem. If we have plenty of experience with the problem, our brains will connect with appropriate experiences and prejudgments. When we have insufficient experience, our brains may connect with misleading experiences or misleading prejudgments.

Left with Prejudgments

We have discussed much of the neuroscience. But it is worth adding one further insight of particular relevance to prejudgments. As explained by V. S. Ramachandran in his book *Phantoms in the Brain: Human Nature and the Architecture of the Mind*, the left side of our brain acts rather as some of the individuals suffering from strong prejudgments described earlier. It sticks to its view of the world, rejecting dissonant information. It is the right side of the brain that challenges the left side to change its view. However, it may not always be successful in doing so.

A dramatic illustration of this comes from patients who have suffered severe damage to the right side of the brain, typically through a stroke. Such patients can persist with the most ridiculous prejudgments, while being otherwise lucid and rational. For example, a proportion of patients deny that they are paralyzed at all. The denial can be extreme. One patient, for example, when confronted with her paralyzed arm, claimed that it belonged to her brother. Another, when asked to clap her hands, waved the good, right hand in the air and claimed that she was clapping with both hands.

This denial, termed *anosognosia*, only exists if the right side of the brain is damaged. Ramachandran suggests that the reason for this behavior is that "the left hemisphere's job is to create a belief system or model and to fold new experiences into that belief system."[12] The left side of our brain has to update its belief structure when new information is received and accepted. But suppose we have one piece of data that seems to contradict what we know—for example, that one-half of our body is not functioning? It is likely that this piece of data is an anomaly. So our left hemisphere rejects it, causing us to persist with our previous belief.

The right hemisphere of our brain, however, acts as a "devil's advocate, to question the status quo and look for global inconsistencies."[13] It challenges our left side and, when the data becomes overwhelming—for example, when we observe that one-half of our body is no longer moving, it forces a restructuring of the left brain's belief system.

If the right side of the brain ceases to function properly, as in patients with strokes in that hemisphere, the left side can go unchecked and may delude the conscious mind in the dramatic way described above. When our right brain is still functioning, the effects may not be as farcical or dramatic—but the left brain's desire to maintain its belief structure can still anchor our thinking inappropriately.

The left side of our brain appears to provide structure and stability. It is here that prejudgments are stored. Our right side seems to be more interactive and challenging. The relevance for strategic decisions is that our brains are best seen as a set of counterbalancing systems. Parts of the brain promote the prejudgments that enable us to survive in a world where many changes are ephemeral and need to be ignored. Other parts of the brain act as a counterbalance, preventing us from becoming too anchored to one viewpoint. This system generally works well—but not always. Sometimes our left brain, the more conservative one, resists new information and leads us to make a flawed decision.

Identifying Misleading Prejudgments

Prejudgments are our views about what is good and bad and about how things work: they form our theories about the world. Prejudgments may be formed around previous experiences, but they can also come from books or other people or our own thoughts.

Spotting prejudgments is critical. In our database of flawed decisions, misleading prejudgments had a "major" or "some" impact in over 80 percent of cases. The types of misleading prejudgment we most frequently spotted in our research were.[14]

- **Judgments about the situation.** These can cause managers to frame the situation they face in a way that influences their decision. For example, prejudgments often cause managers to frame a situation as an opportunity or a threat, or as important or unimportant. Wallace judged Davey's work as a threat and responded accordingly—rejecting the assessment that Davey might be correct and Eglinton a fraud.

- **Judgments about options.** Russell prejudged that managing the business for cash was not an option. Hoover prejudged that spending more government money was not an option. Wallace prejudged that it was not possible that mediums could be a fake.

- **Judgments about objectives or criteria.** Growth strategies are often developed against a prejudgment that growth is essential. Market entry strategies are often influenced by a prejudgment that the company must have 100 percent control. This leads to fewer joint ventures and alliances. With hindsight, Russell commented that Boots "should not have done so much [of the health-care services strategy] ourselves."[15]

- **Judgments about our abilities.** We are often overconfident about what we can do. Russell presumed that Boots managers would be able to develop successful service businesses.

- **Judgments about likely outcomes.** It is not unusual to hear leaders say, "We tried that ten years ago, and it failed," or "If we do this, they will do that." President Hoover judged that a deficit would have severe negative consequences, and so stuck to the view that any solution to the economic crisis must be constrained by the need to balance the budget.

Every decision maker is likely to have many prejudgments. Fortunately, we do not need to list them all and then test each for its misleading qualities. As with misleading experiences, we can focus only on those situations where the decision maker is facing some unfamiliar uncertainties. It is only when the decision involves uncertainties of which the decision maker has insufficient knowledge that prejudgments are likely to be misleading.

As with misleading experiences, we can identify misleading prejudgments by asking ourselves a few questions:

1. What are the main uncertainties involved in this decision?

2. Have the main decision makers prejudged any of these uncertainties?

3. Are the prejudgments well supported by objective evidence? If not, they may be misleading.

In the health-care services decision, Steve Russell faced many important uncertainties. What will be the future profitability in these service areas? How will customers respond to the Boots brand in these areas? How will competitors react? Will professionals in these areas want to work for a large public company? Will Boots managers prove to be capable at managing these slightly different businesses? (Note: If we need to analyze more rigorously the types of uncertainties that might be subject to a prejudgment, we can use the list described earlier: judgments about the uncertainties to do with the situation, the options, the objectives or criteria, our abilities, or the likely outcomes.)

Russell had also clearly prejudged some of these uncertainties. He was confident that profits could be made in health-care services. He was confident the Boots brand would be well received. He was also, as it turned out, overconfident about the ability of Boots managers to run these new businesses.

So the next question is about whether there was sufficient objective evidence to support these prejudgments. We know that a good deal of work had been done on the acceptability of the Boots brand. Hence we would have had little concern about this judgment being misleading. However, there was little evidence that large public companies could make profits in these businesses or that Boots managers would be good at managing them. Both of these prejudgments therefore are potentially misleading: they should be identified as red flags. We are not suggesting that Russell was remiss because he failed to assemble objective evidence for either of these uncertainties. In fact, it would probably not have been possible given the nature of the uncertainties. What we are suggesting is that he may have prejudged these uncertainties in a way that misled him.

While we offer an analytical approach to identifying prejudgments—the three questions above—we also recognize that in many cases, the prejudgment is staring us in the face in the form of a favored option or bias toward one or more objectives. In Russell's case, we hardly need to do the analysis of uncertainties, since he had clearly prejudged that health-care services was a good strategy and that growth was the prime objective.

Use Prejudgments Judiciously

To recap, when we prejudge a situation, we are on our way to believing we are right, when we may well be wrong. Some prejudgments will be supported by reasonable evidence and are justified. Indeed, it is rare that we can make a decision without calling on some prejudgments. However, other prejudgments may be misleading. They may have been valid in some previous situation, but they are not valid in the current situation. Or they may be just plain wrong. When we spot these potentially misleading prejudgments—these red flags—we need to strengthen the decision process in a targeted way to combat the risk that they will lead us to a bad decision.

Misleading prejudgments are among the most powerful causes of bad decisions we have uncovered in our research. This is because they can be attached to powerful emotional tags, which may have been strengthened over time. The initial emotional tag associated with a judgment can be strong either because of the preexisting emotional tags connected to the situation or because the decision maker needed to generate additional emotion around the judgment in order to commit to action. Over time, as the decision maker finds confirmatory evidence, the commitment to the judgment may then become stronger. The result can be a powerful bias in favor of the prejudgment—and a strong resistance to challenges. Hence we need to pay special attention to long-standing prejudgments. But whether prejudgments are long-standing or more recent, we need to recognize how easily they can mislead our thinking.

SEVEN

Inappropriate Self-Interest

WHEN ENRON CORPORATION collapsed in 2001, it became an internationally visible symbol of the dangers of excessive self-interest.

Enron, as many readers will recall, created a network of offshore companies whose purpose was to make Enron look more profitable than it actually was. The scheme worked for a while until the company started into a downward spiral and the corporate officers had to work harder and harder to hide the growing difference between actual and reported performance. Finally, it all came apart, the share price collapsed, and, in December 2001, Enron sought Chapter 11 bankruptcy protection.

The Enron debacle caused an enormous outrage, not simply because of the misreporting of profits, but also because of the way its senior officers had benefited at the expense of Enron's shareholders, employees, pensioners, customers, and suppliers. One of the most infuriating examples was Andrew Fastow, Enron's chief financial officer (CFO), who, along with a few of his cronies, arranged for a number of transactions with Enron that netted them at least $42 million on an initial investment that totaled just $161,000.[1]

Fastow was hardly alone, however. In August 2000, when Enron's stock price hit $90, its highest value ever, many of Enron's executives— who knew all about the company's losses—quietly began selling their stock. However, they continued to publicly predict that the stock could reach highs of $130 or more and encouraged investors to keep buying.[2] As the executives sold their shares, the share price began to drop. Still, company officials and analysts recommended that investors continue to buy, or at least hold their shares, because the stock price was sure to rebound in the near future. Ken Lay, Enron's chairman, was later accused of selling over $70 million worth of stock just before Enron went bankrupt, money he used to repay substantial cash advances he had received from the company.[3]

Whatever your beliefs about the factors that led to Enron's demise, it stands out as an iconic story of self-interest and its corrosive effect on decision making. It is, however, extreme, and we might be tempted to think that self-interest is a rare influence on decision making, limited to a few dishonest or misguided people. Not true. In fact, the impact of self-interest is much more pervasive. It can affect the decisions of the most thoughtful and upstanding leaders. It can influence our judgment even when we are trying to prevent it from doing so.

As we will explore later, the reason why self-interest is such a pervasive influence is that it is particularly difficult for decision makers to be self-aware about how their personal interests are affecting their choices. While all decision making operates to some extent below the level of consciousness, we are particularly prone to screening the effects of self-interest from our conscious mind. It is very difficult for decision makers to compensate for a bias that they are unaware of. The implication is that we should be skeptical of the ability of decision makers to guard against the effects of their own self-interest.[4]

Before describing further case examples where self-interest affected strategic decisions, we will first review some of the existing research that provides evidence for the pervasive and unconscious nature of self-interest.

Self-Interest Beats Objectivity

Do you believe that the unsuccessful party in a legal suit should pay the costs of the other party? According to the results of a survey published in *US News and World Report*, it depends on where your interests lie. When asked, "If someone sues you and you win the case, should he pay your legal costs?" 85 percent of the respondents answered yes. But when asked, "If you sue someone and lose the case, should you pay his costs?" only 44 percent answered yes.[5] Why such different perspectives? Stated simply, because people are highly susceptible to the influence of self-interest—even when they are trying to be objective.

Let's examine this notion in a little more detail. Max Bazerman, of Harvard Business School, has conducted extensive research into the psychology of conflicts of interest, including the role of self-interest in decision making. He designed one experiment that was intended to assess the objectivity of external corporate auditors. An auditor is supposed to serve shareholders, by providing an objective and unbiased review of a company's accounts. In practice, however, the self-interest of the audit firm can come into play. If the auditors deliver a favorable report, the company's management may be more likely to rehire their firm to do the same work next year.

Bazerman's experiment involved 139 experienced auditors at one of the largest accounting firms in the United States. They were asked to evaluate the accounts of a fictional company that we'll call firm A and to determine whether they were in compliance with generally accepted accounting principles (GAAP). Half of the auditors were told that they had been hired by the management of firm A to act as auditors. The other half were told that they had been hired by another company, firm B, seeking to trade with firm A. If the auditors were able to be truly impartial, the average results from the two groups of auditors should have been the same. However, in practice, those who were told that they had been employed by firm A were 30 percent more likely to find that the accounting behind firm A's financial reports complied with GAAP than those employed by firm B.

Bazerman's conclusion is that auditors are not capable of providing an objective assessment when they have a personal motivation for choosing one interpretation of the data over another. The conditions of the experiment should have minimized the chances of their being biased—the client was fictional (so the auditors would not feel a personal connection to any individuals at firm A) and did not offer the prospect of any real income or chance for reemployment. The auditors were explicitly asked to provide an impartial judgment. Nevertheless, they proved susceptible to self-interest. As Bazerman comments, "The evidence suggests that even the possibility of a hypothetical relationship between an auditor and a client distorts the auditor's judgments. One can only imagine the degree of distortion that must exist in a long-standing relationship involving millions of dollars in ongoing revenues."[6] Bazerman's findings, of course, were admirably underlined by the lack of objectivity applied by the audit firm Arthur Andersen when assessing Enron's accounts.[7]

Auditors are not the only people whose decisions can be distorted by self-interest—any kind of decision maker is likely to be similarly affected. For example, a large number of studies conducted by independent medical researchers, but financed by the pharmaceutical industry, report results that are favorable to the financial sponsors. In one study, clinical trials on breast cancer treatments sponsored by pharmaceutical companies were found to be significantly more likely to report that the drug treatments were effective than when the studies were independently financed. In another study, 84 percent of the trials that had drug industry sponsorship reported success, while only 54 percent of independent trials did so.[8] The same correlation has been documented in other medical trials: for stroke, for heart disease, and for psychiatric disorders, among others.[9]

Might this just be a case of a few bad apples spoiling the barrel? It appears not. Most of us will bend the rules to serve our personal interests—as illustrated by an experiment conducted by Dan Ariely and described in his excellent book *Predictably Irrational*.[10] Ariely gave students a test consisting of 50 multiple-choice questions. However, the test was designed to be subtly different for different groups of students. The first group was required to transfer their answers from their worksheet to a scoring sheet. They then handed the scoring sheet in to a proctor at the front of the room. The proctor gave them 10¢ for every correct answer. The average student scored 32.6 out of 50.

Other students were given exactly the same test and the same incentives—but allowed to cheat in a variety of ways. For example, the correct answers were indicated on the scoring sheet so that the student could fill in the correct answer rather than the answer that they had originally marked on their worksheet. The resulting score from these students was significantly higher: over 36 correct answers out of 50.

The main conclusion from this experiment was that people will be motivated by their self-interest—in this case, cheating when they can get away with it. However, there was an interesting second conclusion. Rather than a few students cheating a lot, it turned out that most students cheated a bit.[11] The implication: most decisions makers will be susceptible to the distorting effects of self-interest.

The conclusion from these examples is that we are susceptible to the effects of self-interest—even when we are trying to be objective. How members of the public view who should pay legal costs depends on whether it is they or someone else that will benefit—even when they are asked to provide an objective viewpoint. Auditors' advice and the results of academics' studies are affected by who is paying for them, even though objectivity is a raison d'être of both professions. Most people, rather than a minority, took the chance to cheat in Dan Ariely's test. In the next section, we present evidence suggesting *why* self-interest has such a powerful influence on decision making—even when we try to be objective.

Unconsciously Self-Interested

Did the respondents to the survey on who should pay for legal costs realize that their answers were influenced by their self-interest? Probably not. In fact, it's likely they thought their answers were perfectly reasonable. When we carry out similar surveys with executives, those involved always laugh when we present the results, because they realize that they have been "had"—they realize that they were, in fact, influenced by the way the question was put, and that they were unaware of the biasing effect of self-interest.

The evidence from our experience and from other researchers suggests that decision makers are far more affected by self-interest than they claim and realize. It is this lack of awareness of the effects of self-interest that makes it particularly important to diagnose, because an unconscious influence is much harder for the decision maker to guard against.

In chapters 2 and 3, we discussed how our brains often operate at an unconscious level. As we evaluate a decision—for example, whether we or the other party should pay legal costs—the two options will unconsciously be tagged with emotions that guide our choice. The option in which we pay costs will feel unattractive, and the option in which we have costs paid to us will feel attractive. Although our reasoning, conscious mind subsequently has the chance to think about the choice and overrule these feelings, the brain is already focused in favor of the attractive option and against the unattractive option. It is this unconscious involvement of self-interest in our decision making that makes it particularly influential on which option we go for. No doubt many of the auditors described earlier would have reconsidered their decision if they had been aware of the effects of their self-interest.

While the effect of self-interest on strategic decisions cannot easily be researched under controlled conditions, there is a body of relevant investigation that confirms its unconscious nature.

For a controlled test of the effect of unconscious self-interest on our decisions, consider the following experiment, in which participants were asked to play the role of either the defendant or the plaintiff in a mock legal case. The plaintiff was suing the defendant for damages following an automobile accident. To simulate real life, each party was offered an incentive if they could reach a favorable negotiated settlement rather than take the case to court. The plaintiffs, therefore, had a self-interest in persuading the defendants that a high payout was appropriate, and the defendants a self-interest in persuading the plaintiffs that a low payout was appropriate.

To prepare for the negotiation, the participants were given a common set of materials about the facts of the case and told to review them. The case was a real one that had already been settled by a judge, and thus the court outcome was known but not shared with the participants. Before they negotiated with each other, the participants were asked to make a private estimate of what they thought the actual judge had awarded the plaintiff. To ensure that their estimates were not deliberately biased, the participants were offered a small bonus if their estimate was close to the actual settlement made by the judge in the real case.

Consider the situation. It should not make a difference whether the participant is a plaintiff or a defendant—either way they get a bonus if they accurately estimate the actual settlement made by the actual judge. However, the plaintiffs' estimate of the judge's actual award was still much higher than that of the people playing the defendants: $38,953 versus $24,426.[12] When asked what they thought a fair award would be, the plaintiffs also came up with a value that was about twice as high as the defendants' ($37,028 versus $19,318).

The explanation offered by the researchers is that the participants' estimates of the actual reward were distorted by their underlying self-interest—which they termed a *self-serving bias*. For example, plaintiffs had a self-interest in persuading the defendants that the award should be very high. When asked to come up with an unbiased, private estimate of the actual award or a fair award, they nevertheless guessed twice as high as the defendants did. Their underlying self-interest in the outcome of the case created a significant bias that they appear to have been unaware of and thus unable to compensate for.[13]

Particularly interesting insights into the unconscious nature of self-interest came from the researchers' attempts to reduce the level of bias. The experiment was run again, and this time some of the participants attended a brief coaching session, during which they were advised about the risks of self-serving biases and how such biases might distort their decisions. But the coaching did not work as planned. As one of the researchers put it, "The intervention was successful insofar as the individuals became convinced that their negotiating opponent would be biased, but the individuals themselves believed that they would not be. Moreover, when individuals did concede that they might be somewhat biased, they tended to drastically underestimate how strong their bias would be."[14] Even after coaching, the participants were unable to detect the distorting effect of their own self-interest.

Some participants were asked to write a short essay arguing the opponents' case as strongly as possible, with the intention of helping them see that they might be biased in their own assessments. But this had the opposite effect—*increasing* the amount of bias.[15] It was only when the participants were asked to list the weaknesses in their own case that the degree of bias was reduced. The implication is that we are unconscious of the effects of self-interest on our decision making—and it takes a lot to make us think again and counterbalance our own biases.[16] We understand intellectually that people can be biased by their self-interest—but find it extremely difficult to accept that this is true about ourselves.

More anecdotal research provides additional evidence that self-interest operates unconsciously. For example, in a study of medical residents in health-care organizations in the United States, 61 percent of the respondents said that "promotions don't influence my practice"—meaning that when prescribing medicines, they were not influenced by the promotional efforts of drug makers. Only 16 percent of them, however, believed that the statement was true of other physicians. As it turns out, evidence from other studies generally confirms that promotions do indeed affect prescribing practices. One study showed that physicians who attended a seminar run by a drug company wrote more prescriptions for the drugs discussed there than they had before the seminar. But nineteen of the twenty physicians who attended the seminar denied that it would have an influence on their behavior.[17]

The tendency to argue for our own interests—but not to realize that we are doing so—runs deep within even the most rational mind. When coauthors are asked what proportion of the effort they were responsible for in producing a book, the total typically adds up to over 100 percent.

The same effect has been observed to be true of those supposed paragons of rationality, Nobel Prize winners. After Frederick Banting and John Macleod won the Nobel Prize for their discovery of insulin, Banting contended that his partner had been more of a hindrance than a help. In turn, when Macleod made speeches describing the discovery, he failed to mention that he had a partner at all. It is possible, of course, that such individuals deliberately overstated their achievements. However, it appears more likely that they truly believed what they were saying. The tendency to present one's own contribution as being more significant than it really was has been found in situations as diverse as athletics, fund-raising, and marriage.[18] For example, when married couples describe their individual contributions to household chores, both men and women overestimate their contribution.[19]

Evolutionary Insights

Why is it so difficult for us to be aware of the effects of our personal interests on our decision making? Evolutionary psychologists suggest that we evolved like this because the best way of persuading others of our objectivity is to believe it ourselves.

Evolutionary psychologists argue that we have evolved as social animals who are members of a group. Within a group, there are always disputes—for example, over who should have what share of the available food. Our ancestors would have benefited from being successful in arguing their position convincingly—doing so would have increased their chances of gaining more food and other resources. One of the best ways of being successful in argument is to appear sincere and be persistent in arguing one's position, and doing so is easier if we genuinely believe that our argument is right. To do so, it is better that we are unaware of the influence that our self-interest is having on our argument, and that we think we are arguing on a purely objective basis. As a result, we will tend to argue in favor of outcomes that benefit ourselves while remaining unaware that we are doing so.[20] We may truly believe we are right, when in fact we are wrong.

Not only do we suppress the knowledge that self-interest is influencing our decisions, we may go a step further and convince ourselves that we are using fair or even altruistic criteria in making a decision.[21] However, fairness acts as a screen. What we see as fair is biased by our self-interest.[22] Linda Babcock and George Lowenstein, part of the research group that conducted the role-playing of defendants and plaintiffs described earlier, concluded that "both parties' notions of fairness will tend to gravitate toward settlements that favor themselves. They will not only view these settlements as fair, but believe that their personal conception of fairness is impartial."[23]

Returning to the Enron example, when the CFO, Andy Fastow, was told that he would have to formally give up all his interests in one of the funds from which he had made tens of millions of dollars, he reportedly threw a tantrum. He later apologized, explaining that he had created the partnership, and selling it was very emotional for him. No doubt many outside observers would see Fastow's resistance to giving up his interest in the partnership as a clear example of the effects of self-interest. But Fastow himself seems to have seen it as being more like a parent separating from a child.

It is impossible to prove what Fastow's motivation really was—but this is the point. Righteous indignation, such as Fastow suggested he experienced, may have been screening less "righteous" motives. But it is so convincingly done that the underlying motivation is hard to prove. Only by convincing themselves of their impartiality do decision makers have any chance of also convincing others.

Another way for our brain to disguise self-interest is for us to characterize the *opposing* viewpoint as being self-interested or irrational. An example comes from the cold war, in which neither side was prepared to sacrifice enough of its own interests to reach agreement on an arms deal, but both sides explained this by saying that the other side had been rigid and obstructionist. At the conclusion of a historic meeting to discuss arms reduction, President Reagan told reporters, "We came to Iceland to advance the cause of peace . . . and although we put on the table the most far-reaching arms control proposal in history, the General Secretary rejected it." On the same day, Gorbachev stated, "I proposed an urgent meeting here because we had something to propose . . . the Americans came to this meeting empty handed." Researchers who have closely examined the motives of each individual have concluded that their comments were more than rhetoric—both individuals genuinely believed that they had been prepared to put aside at least some of their own interests and that the other side had been inflexible in not doing so.[24] Reagan and Gorbachev appear not only to have been unconscious of the influence of their own interests; they also believed they were behaving honorably by offering significant concessions—while the other party was not. We have already noted that the participants in the mock legal case were quite able to see how their opponents might be biased— while at the same time assuming that they themselves would not be.

How Self-Interest Affects Strategic Decisions

Inappropriate self-interest contributed to a flawed strategic decision in two-thirds of our cases. A couple of examples illustrate its beguiling and unconscious influence.

The performance of a European subsidiary of a major packaged goods company had declined sharply, and a new managing director had been appointed. The new managing director then recruited Mike from his previous post as marketing director for a German company. One of the decisions facing Mike was whether to keep or fire one of his most important direct reports: a brand manager who controlled 35 percent of the business, with revenues of $190 million. The evidence suggested that the individual concerned was not up to the job. He had not been able to lead and delegate effectively. The performance of the brands under his management was poor. Having an effective brand manager in this position was critical if Mike was to turn around the business. Mike felt in his gut that the individual was not up to the job.

Nevertheless, Mike opted to keep the brand manager in place. Mike now believes that his decision was flawed. The individual did not deliver and left the company, but only after six months of continued poor performance by the brands involved. After the debacle, Mike's boss told him that he had thought Mike should have made the decision to fire him earlier. (His boss had not intervened because he wanted Mike to make and live with the decision.) When we interviewed him some time afterward, Mike felt that he had the information required to make the right choice, but failed to do so.

As we discussed the case with him, we reviewed a number of possible causes, such as misleading experiences or prejudgments. However, as we talked, Mike suddenly stopped in midsentence. "My past experience guided my decision to some extent—but there was also an emotional reaction . . . the building is on fire . . . can I cope? How will I be seen? I was led more by my heart than my head. I wanted to create the right impression for myself."

As we continued our discussion with Mike, he clarified in his own mind why he had made this bad decision. Three types of personal interest influenced him. Each conflicted with the interests of the company and was thus an inappropriate influence on the decision.

The first type of self-interest was to look good in the eyes of his boss, who was pushing for an early improvement in performance. Even if keeping his subordinate was a bad decision over the longer term, holding on to him might help Mike get through the next few months. Of course, Mike could have gone back to his boss to discuss whether it would be better to get in a new direct report, even if short-term performance suffered slightly—but Mike felt wary of such a conversation so recently after having been hired. In hindsight it might have been good to have had that conversation—but at the time it didn't feel like something that Mike wanted to do.

The second type of personal interest was Mike's desire to be popular. The individual concerned was liked by many of his team—firing him would make Mike unpopular. That wouldn't necessarily make Mike less effective as a manager, but life would be lonelier.

The third was lifestyle. He wanted to be able to spend time with his family, particularly as they had just moved from one country to another.

Keeping the existing manager meant that Mike would be able to delegate more of his workload. Firing him meant spending extra hours in the office until a new manager could be appointed.

We are not saying that self-interest should never be a criterion for decision making. Rather, we are using this example to illustrate how inappropriate self-interest can influence a decision without its influence being recognized at the time. If Mike had recognized how self-interest was influencing his decision, he might have been able to think of ways to remove his troublesome subordinate while reducing the costs to himself. For example, he could have investigated ways to shift some of his other responsibilities onto others while he filled in for his missing subordinate. He could have put special effort into explaining his decision to members of his team. He could have discussed with his boss the time pressure he felt under and how it was pushing him to make a decision that went against his gut feeling. But because he was not conscious of the influence of his self-interest, he instead persuaded himself that it was better to keep the subordinate, when the information he had indicated the opposite.

It was only in hindsight that Mike was able to see how his decision was being influenced by personal interests. In Mike's words, he was "overwhelmed by emotions." His self-interest triggered feelings that led him to make a bad decision—even though he was trying to be objective. Indeed, he had not been fully aware of how his feelings were manipulating his thinking until we talked about it well after the event—until then, some of the reasons for his decision had lain buried inside his head and heart.

In another case, Marc was the managing director of the French subsidiary of an international manufacturer of packaging machinery. He was considering whether or not to acquire a company that had a near monopoly on manufacturing a specialized type of food packaging machine. While the company had a strong position in the market, there were several warning signs that it was a risky investment. The business was highly dependent on sales to one large meat processing company. Because the machinery was a form of capital investment, sales tended to be highly cyclical. The management team had recently lost some of its more talented designers and marketers, and performance was flagging. The current owners of the business were keen to sell.

These risks were particularly an issue because Marc had committed to his head office that he would deliver relatively stable performance. The previous year, Marc had personally persuaded the head office to provide additional investment to his subsidiary for low-risk acquisitions, and so his reputation was at stake.

As the transaction progressed, some members of Marc's supervisory board voiced their concerns about the proposed acquisition. Despite this, Marc went ahead. A few months later, following the discovery of bovine spongiform encephalopathy (BSE), or mad cow disease, in French cattle, the meat processing customer announced that it was putting discretionary capital expenditure, including the packaging machines manufactured by Marc's company, on hold. The management team was unable to deal with the dramatic drop-off in demand. Profits plunged into the red. Marc's superiors were shocked, and Marc's career received a large black mark.

Marc described why he thought he had made a flawed decision. "I was under pressure to do this deal for my own interest. If I went ahead, then the costs incurred in auditing and due diligence of the company would be capitalized and added to the cost of the investment. If I backed out, then they would all be charged to my office as an expense. Because we had been pursuing this company for a while, those costs were quite significant—and I guess I was influenced by that. I had an annual target to hit—and the charge-off would occur at the end of the financial year, leaving me no time to find a way to avoid a big loss. Of course, in the end, doing a bad deal was much worse for my position. I guess self-interest *clouded my judgment*."

"Self-interest clouded my judgment" is a good description of the effect on Marc's decision. He couldn't see at the time how self-interest was leading him astray. It affected his judgment, but he was unaware of the way it was doing so. Only in hindsight and through the process of reflection could he see why he had made a mistake.

Note also that, like Mike, he was particularly influenced by his short-term interests—which were to hit his budget for the year. Short-term pressures can lead us to make choices that are even against our own long-term interests. Recently, neuroscientists have uncovered evidence that this is indeed the case. Our short-term interests can be overly influential in our decisions—triumphing not only over the broader interests involved in the decision (shareholders, other members of the organization, etc.) but even over the long-term interests of the decision maker.

I Want It—*Now*!

Researchers have long noted that people's decisions are particularly biased toward achieving short-term goals—even at the expense of their longer-term self-interests. Those who have studied such behavior suggest that it comes about because we have two very different selves. Our "want" self is focused on the short-term payoff. Our "should" self takes a more balanced, longer-term view of what is best for us.[25] The two selves are constantly in debate about what actions to take. Because we have what researchers have termed *bounded willpower*, our "want" self sometimes wins out over our "should" self.[26] Bounded willpower implies that even when we try hard to satisfy our "should" self, it can be overcome when the short-term temptation is too great.[27]

Recent research in neuroscience has revealed more about the nature of these two selves. Samuel McClure, of the Center for the Study of Brain, Mind and Behavior at Princeton University, working with a team of researchers, scanned the brain of subjects as they were being offered a series of choices between a short-term and a longer-term reward. The researchers found that certain parts of the limbic system, an older part of the brain associated with emotions, was activated only by the prospect of a short-term reward. Parts of the cortex, the outer part of the brain associated with more cognitive thinking, were activated by both the short-term and the longer-term benefits. The relative amount of activity of these two parts of the brain correlated with the choice the subject would make. When the activity in the limbic system was greater than in the cortex, the subject would invariably choose the shorter-term reward.[28]

These results suggest an explanation for why we are often unconscious of the effects of our short-term personal interests on our decisions. People are likely to be less conscious of the powerful effects of such biases, because they arise from a more primitive part of our brain.

The strong influence of short-term interests helps to explain many flawed business decisions. Mike, our marketing director, described his decision to retain his subordinate as "a triumph of the short-term over the long-term interests," going on to rationalize this choice by adding, "Companies are very short term—you do tend to make a reputation for yourself. It (short-term interests) can be very influential, and that is the reality of the business world." Marc risked his reputation with his company because of his desire to hit his short-term targets. "Short-termism" is part of our human nature. It can lead to us making decisions that are not only against the interests of others—they are even against our own interests.

The implication? We must pay particular attention to a decision maker's short-term interests. They can have enormous influence on a decision, even when we see that satisfying them could conflict with the decision maker's long-term interests.

Self-Interest—the Bottom Line

So how does all this affect strategic decision making? Simply put, we will tend to be biased toward choices that are in our own interests—particularly short-term interests—without realizing the full extent to which we are doing so. We will likely be aware of any interests that we have at stake in the decision. We will likely be aware that they are affecting our judgment. But we may not be aware of the full impact of those interests on our decision. For example, business unit managers may be asked to put on a "corporate hat" when sitting on an executive board. However, despite their best efforts, their natural instincts will be to unconsciously factor in their own interests and those of their business units when making decisions. Though they may be utterly convinced that they are putting aside their personal interests, they will be influenced strongly by any such interests that are involved.

Take More Precautions!

We have made the case that self-interest can have a particularly distorting effect on decisions. Unfortunately, people and organizations do not always take sufficient precautions. For example, Professor Bazerman and his colleagues informed the Securities and Exchange Commission (SEC) about the results of their research into the self-interested behavior of independent company auditors. They advised that auditors simply could not be objective when acting within the prevailing system for hiring and engaging them, and made recommendations for ways to increase the auditors' independence. Nevertheless, the SEC did not act upon Bazerman's advice. Similarly, there is a good deal of evidence (as well as common sense) that shows that when doctors receive gifts from pharmaceutical companies, their decision making may be biased in favor of the gift giver. Even so, such gifts are rarely banned.

Why? One reason is that self-interest is in many ways the engine that drives the modern organization and society at large. While it carries the risk of distorting decisions, trying to exclude the influence of self-interest on decision making would be a case of throwing out the baby with the bathwater. Shares and options are granted to managers, such as at Enron, with the intention of motivating them to create shareholder value far in excess of any increase in their personal wealth. Mike's self-interest encouraged him to work hard and perform well for a number of companies—indeed, he was later promoted to be managing director of the business.

Much of economic theory, and, in fact, the entire Western capitalist system, is based on the presumption that self-interest can work for the common good. In the words of the eighteenth-century economist Adam Smith, "It is not from the benevolence of the butcher, the brewer, or the baker, that we can expect our dinner, but from their regard to their own interest."[29]

Paul Lawrence and Nitin Nohria, both professors at Harvard Business School, identify four fundamental human drives in their book *Driven*: to acquire, to bond, to learn, and to defend, all of which have an element of self-interest. Lawrence and Nohria argue that in order to be successful, an organization needs to harness and apply all these drives. That's why self-interest is often accepted as a normal influence in decision making and organizational life in general.[30]

Even when the potential distortions from self-interest are recognized, the steps taken to combat them may be inadequate. For example, in the wake of scandals, such as those at Enron, Tyco, and WorldCom, many advocated an increase in the teaching of ethics to business people and students at business schools. However, the reality we have seen is that a better understanding of ethics is unlikely to affect the unconscious and powerful feelings of self-interest that shape decisions. It would be better to spend more time making people aware of the impossibility of preventing people from being biased by their self-interests, and describing the many practical steps that can counterbalance the inevitable influence of self-interest on decisions.

The implication for avoiding flawed decisions is that we need to be particularly careful to consider the potential threat posed by self-interest, because it is so often considered to be a normal and useful factor in decision-making processes and organizational life. Self-interest provides the motivation that drives individuals to aspire to and achieve success, which we consider to be a positive thing. The danger is that we often overestimate our ability to recognize and eliminate the negative effects of our natural self-interest, and so it can run out of control.

Identifying Inappropriate Self-Interest

Self-interest will always be present. There are few decisions in which we have no personal interests. Fortunately, our personal interests are often aligned with those of the organization. Hence they help us make the right decision. Problems only arise when our personal interests conflict with the interests of the main stakeholders: when this happens, they are inappropriate. So how do we spot self-interests, and how do we decide whether they are likely to be a problem?

The sources of self-interest that most commonly affect decisions include:

- **Achieving financial rewards, job perks, and career advancement.** Enron provides a good example.

- **Hitting particular goals and targets.** Sometimes a decision maker has a particularly influential goal or target—particularly if it is a short-term target. Marc was under pressure to make his annual budget—which influenced him to make a bad investment decision.

- **Enhancing prestige and reputation.** A CEO we know refused to make an acquisition in his last year in office because it would have temporarily diluted earnings per share, and he wanted to retire on an undisputed high note.

- **Being popular.** Mike, the marketing director facing the decision about whether or not to fire his subordinate, did not want to be seen as "Attila the Hun" within the organization.

- **Having fun at work.** By keeping rather than firing his subordinate, Mike was able to spend more time working on the overall strategy for the brand and coaching his team—aspects of the job that he particularly enjoyed.

- **Achieving a better lifestyle.** The CEO of a consulting company we interviewed felt, in hindsight, that he had agreed to the disastrous centralization of the company by an incoming COO partly because it would allow him more time with his family. Bill Agee, CEO of Morrison Knudsen, a major construction company, moved his home to Pebble Beach, California, and ran the company by fax, phone, and weekly briefings with executives who shuttled between Agee's house and the company's headquarters in Boise, Idaho. Why? Agee loved the golf course at Pebble Beach and wanted to be there despite the obvious inefficiencies and extra expenses involved.

Fortunately, we do not need to consider all of a decision maker's self-interests. We are only interested in those areas of self-interest that might inappropriately distort the decision. We can spot inappropriate self-interest by focusing on the options that the decision maker is trying to choose between. By identifying options that are likely to be personally attractive or unattractive, we can spot areas of inappropriate self-interest. The process involves three questions:[31]

1. Are any of the options likely to be particularly attractive or unattractive given the personal interests, particularly the short-term interests of the decision makers?

2. Are these interests likely to conflict with the interests of the main stakeholders?

3. Are any conflicting interests likely to be strong enough to significantly distort the decision?

Let's illustrate this with an example: that of Mike, the new marketing director who faced a decision about whether or not to fire a particular brand manager. Imagine that you are his boss. You want Mike to pick his own team, but you also want to help Mike be objective in his decision.

The first question is whether any of the options are likely to be attractive or unattractive to Mike. In this case, the options are very simple: to keep or to fire his subordinate.

Considering the first of these options, Mike could certainly find keeping his subordinate attractive. It could help him achieve the short-term goals he has been given to turn around the business. If he can turn the employee's performance around it would eliminate the need for him to find and hire a replacement. It would reduce the chance of him being seen as an "Attila" by an already demoralized team. It will allow him to spend more time with his family. (Note: You can use the checklist of sources of self-interest given above to help structure this analysis, if needed). These personal interests suggest that Mike may be biased toward keeping the employee.

Now turn to the second question: are any of Mike's interests likely to conflict with those of the organization? Some will and some won't. Mike's interest in avoiding being seen as "Atilla the Hun" could well conflict with the interests of the business, as could his desire to spend time with his family. Of course, it will not help the business if Mike's subordinates refuse to work with him, or if he suffers from burnout. But it is not appropriate for Mike to keep the subordinate just because it might make him less popular, and he may need to work particularly hard over the next few months, given the pressures of his job.

Mike's short-term interest in hitting his targets appears reasonably aligned with those of the business. However, because you know that short-term interests can have excessive influence in our minds, you may still conclude that this is a red flag condition.

Finally, you turn to the third question. Will any of Mike's interests significantly distort the decision? Clearly, any one of these interests could bias Mike's thinking. In other words there are some red flags here. You will never be certain whether Mike's thinking is biased. But you can be certain that some inappropriate self-interest exists and this is sufficient for you to raise a red flag.

There are of course some balancing forces on Mike. For example, he also has an interest in making sure he has the best possible team. So you may want to explore the issue with Mike to understand better what factors he is putting most weight on. But beware. Mike may be influenced by self-interest without knowing it. If you have had little experience of managing Mike, you will want to be cautious, raise red flags and put in place some balancing influences.

This example illustrates a common feature when identifying red flags. Some are very obvious—but for others you may not have all the information you need. By going through the questions and checklists provided you can identify *possible* red flags and learn where further investigation may be helpful. You can't be sure whether a decision maker is suffering from distorted thinking and you can't eliminate the risk of a flawed decision—but you can improve your odds. Further approaches for doing so are discussed in chapter 10 and also on our Web site, www.thinkagain-book.com.

———————

In conclusion, self-interest shows up in varying guises. The type of self-interest we saw in the Enron scandal makes big headlines. However, the more common and relevant type is more morally ambiguous. While it does not necessarily make news, it has an influence on countless business decisions, large and small. It influences decision makers even when they are trying to be objective. Indeed, the decision maker often believes he or she is making a rational decision and may even convince others of the reasonableness of the arguments. All along, however, self-interest is at work behind the scenes. This can lead decision makers to underestimate its effect—but they do so at their peril.

Harnessing self-interest is necessary to drive decision making and organizational life in general. What we need to worry about is inappropriate self-interest, when the interests of the decision maker are in conflict with those of other stakeholders in the decision and might significantly distort the decision. Inappropriate self-interest is the third of our red flag conditions under which we need to strengthen the decision process.

EIGHT

Inappropriate Attachments

IN MARCH 2005, Paul Wolfowitz was nominated to take over as head of the World Bank by George W. Bush, president of the United States.[1] Wolfowitz, who did his undergraduate work at Cornell and earned a PhD in political science from the University of Chicago, was serving as deputy secretary of defense at the time.[2] While negotiating his contract, Wolfowitz disclosed that he was involved in a romantic relationship with Shaha Ali Riza, who served as senior communications officer on the staff of the World Bank. The relationship violated a World Bank rule regarding "real or apparent" conflicts of interest, so Wolfowitz offered to excuse himself from any personnel decisions that might pertain to Riza.[3]

The matter was referred to the bank's ethics committee (EC), but it had not ruled on the matter by the time Wolfowitz started work on June 1, 2005. The ethics committee, which was composed of three executive directors of the bank, unanimously decided that Wolfowitz's offer to excuse himself from this decision was not sufficient to alleviate the potential conflict of interest.[4] The bank's rules required that conflicted parties had to be situated in the organization such that no direct or indirect supervision would exist between them, and that they could have no professional contact. But as president of the bank, Wolfowitz did, in fact, have indirect supervision over Riza.

Wolfowitz was perturbed by the decision. He believed that his offer to excuse himself from personnel decisions relating to Riza more than satisfied the rule and eliminated the potential conflict.[5] As a consequence, he chose not to eliminate his professional contacts with Riza.[6] Since Wolfowitz would not solve the issue himself, the EC was forced to evaluate the actions it could recommend, based on the bank's extensive guidelines for such situations:[7]

> **Reassignment.** Riza could be transferred to a different position at the bank, where she would no longer be under Wolfowitz's supervision. However, given Wolfowitz's position, there were few jobs of similar grade that were outside his sphere of authority. Riza's career path might be affected.

> **Mutually agreed separation.** Riza could leave the bank, agree not to make any future claims against it, and receive a lump sum payment of about $65,000 (based on one month's salary for each year of service).

> **External service.** Riza could take an assignment with a non-bank organization, such as a member government or client. These external assignments were usually for purposes of enhancing relations, acquiring new skills, or providing technical assistance to outside groups. These employees were generally paid by the bank as if they were internal staffers.

The ethics committee did not believe that reassignment within the bank would work and doubted that Riza would agree to a mutually agreed separation, so it recommended external service as the best option for her. It also suggested that she be given a promotion to the next job grade, in recognition of the career disruption the change in position might cause. (The EC felt this was justified since Riza was already in line for a promotion in her current department.) As the committee could not be directly involved in staff discussions, it then ordered

Wolfowitz to refer the matter to Xavier Coll, vice president of human resources.[8]

At Wolfowitz's insistence, Coll met with Riza in early August to hammer out an agreement. Of course, Wolfowitz should not have been involved in the process at all—remember, he had already stated his intent to excuse himself from any personnel matters involving Riza. Riza told Coll that she was being forced into the transfer as the result of a conflict that she did not cause. Nevertheless, she no doubt recognized the difficulty of her situation and so put her efforts into getting a better deal. She demanded the promotion, a $50,000 raise, guaranteed 8 percent annual pay increases, and guaranteed promotions in five and ten years.[9]

Coll felt these terms were extraordinary. The raise associated with such a promotion was normally capped at $20,000, annual increases were typically around 3 percent, and there was absolutely no provision for guaranteed promotions.[10] Coll reported on the negotiations to Wolfowitz, who overstepped his authority once again and directed Coll to accept Riza's terms. Coll found himself in an extremely difficult position but did manage to gain one modification to the package: Riza would have to be evaluated by a panel of her peers (selected with her approval) for future promotions.

Wolfowitz was still not pleased. He sent a memo to Coll, detailing the terms of the agreement that he thought were right, expressing his displeasure with the whole situation, and arguing that his offer to remove himself from the decision should have been enough.[11] He seemed unable to recognize that it was his decision to join the bank that triggered the problem in the first place and, even more important, that it was his personal attachment to Riza that was leading him to make a series of inappropriate decisions.[12]

In a separate conversation, Wolfowitz forbade Coll from conferring with the bank's general counsel, or anyone else, about the Riza matter. He later explained that he made this demand because he felt that the general counsel was conflicted and could not advise both the bank and its president. This was a curious explanation, however, because it would only make sense if the bank and the president were at odds with one another—that is, if the president were acting for his own (or Riza's) benefit, to the detriment of the bank, which Wolfowitz vehemently denied he was doing.[13] Even so, Coll complied with the demand, and in September 2005, he signed a letter of agreement with the terms named by Riza and approved by Wolfowitz.[14]

Even before the deal was signed, Wolfowitz wrote to the ethics committee informing its members that Riza had taken an external assignment and the issue was therefore resolved. He did not offer any details of the agreement, but hinted that Riza was being forced out of the bank and that her career would likely be damaged through no fault of her own.[15]

That seemed to be the end of the matter. Then, in January 2006, a group of World Bank employees, acting anonymously and identifying themselves as "John Smith," contacted the ethics committee and the board of directors with allegations that Wolfowitz had been involved in misconduct and ethical lapses. The letter from "Smith" contained accurate details about Riza's salary and promotion deal, and claimed that its allegations were "widely known throughout the Bank and beyond," and that "these rumors cause great harm to staff morale, and immense damage to the World Bank's credibility."[16]

The EC reviewed the allegations and decided that "Smith's" letter contained no new information regarding Riza and that the financial details of her compensation were outside the purview of the committee. The EC informed Wolfowitz that it would take no action regarding the letter from "John Smith."[17] Again, the matter went dormant.

But then, in late March, the issue exploded when the *Washington Post* published an article about the whole messy situation, particularly Riza's salary.[18] Wolfowitz's spokesman had been interviewed for the article and had claimed that "arrangements concerning Shaha Riza were made at the direction of the Bank's board of directors," which was simply not the case. Other media outlets jumped on the story, and it spread like wildfire. On April 6, the directors of the bank formed an ad hoc group to investigate the allegations of ethical lapses and managerial wrongdoing.[19]

Wolfowitz went on the defensive. He claimed that he had understood the recommendation from the ethics committee as a directive to him to deal with the Riza issue immediately and personally.[20] However, this interpretation thrust Wolfowitz into the middle of the very conflict of interest that the bank had been so earnestly trying to avoid. Wolfowitz justified the $50,000 raise by claiming that Riza had been inappropriately denied promotion in prior years and hence was deserving of compensatory pay. This, too, was disingenuous, since such a claim should have been handled through the appropriate HR processes.[21] Wolfowitz went on to argue that he was only acting on the EC's ruling. Both Wolfowitz and Riza proclaimed that the whole situation was not their fault and they never liked the deal anyway. Finally, however, in a statement to the World Bank, Wolfowitz admitted that he should not have been involved in the details of the negotiation with Riza.[22]

On May 14, 2007, the ad hoc investigatory group submitted its report. It found that Wolfowitz had indeed violated staff rules, breached his contract, and ignored the requirement to avoid any conflict of interest. Three days later, the board announced that it had accepted Wolfowitz's assertion that he "acted ethically and in good faith in what he believed were the best interests of the institution." The board also announced that it had accepted Wolfowitz's resignation, effective June 30, 2007, and thanked him for his service to the bank.[23]

The story of Paul Wolfowitz and the series of remarkably poor decisions he made in this process is obviously one that highlights his emotional attachment to Shaha Ali Riza. Clearly, he was a leader caught in a conflict of interest of his own making who, rather than defuse the problem in a manner consistent with the rules of his organization, did the opposite. Remarkably, he not only sought to further the interests of his girlfriend, he also took advantage of every opportunity to complain about his predicament.

Personal attachments surround us and can have a major role in any decision, sometimes to our extreme detriment. Our research found that attachments, as valuable as they can be for many aspects of our lives, can also trap us without our realizing it. Attachments are very important to consider. They bring meaning and joy to our lives—they include attachments to our friends and families, to communities, to places, and even to objects that have taken on significance for us. It would be virtually impossible not to be affected by these attachments as we make decisions, but, under certain circumstances, they can cause us to make flawed decisions—as Paul Wolfowitz discovered, too late.

Do emotional attachments push smart leaders to make bad decisions? The Wolfowitz story is a rather extreme and public example that suggests they can. But attachments need not be so intimate to have an influence on decision making.

Astonishing Attachments

Even those of us involved in deep research into flawed decision making are prone to irrational attachments. When Andrew Campbell cofounded Ashridge Strategic Management Centre, as a subsidiary of the Ashridge business school, one of the first things he did was personally commission the design and development of the logo and notepaper for the new subsidiary. He was well pleased with the process, the individual identity that resulted, and the subsequent growth of the new entity. Two years later, a review of the Ashridge brand resulted in a decision, at the parent company level, to create a shared logo and common identity for all units of the group. This resulted in a particularly tense telephone call between Andrew and the head of marketing for the group. Andrew argued for an exception to the process of standardization because he felt that the subsidiary would suffer if it did not present an independent image.

The call became quite heated, as the head of marketing pressed her case and Andrew continued to argue for the logo he had designed. At last Andrew realized he was going to lose the argument and ended the call. As soon as he put down the phone, he burst into tears. His attachment to the logo was that strong and that irrational. Within a few weeks, it was obvious to him not only that the new logo was superior to the old, but that the benefits of standardization far outweighed the benefits of differentiation. However, before the call he had not been aware of the depth of his emotional attachment to the logo and all that it represented. Andrew's attachment to a logo powerfully influenced his ability to make a decision about the best way to market the center.

In both of these stories, attachments were formed as the result of powerful emotional experiences and produced strong emotional tags that had the ability to drive decision making off the rails. Attachments that conflicted with other stakeholders' interests contributed to almost half of the examples of flawed decisions in our case database. For this reason, it's important to understand which attachments we need to look out for and how they can influence decisions.

Attachments form an astonishing range. From lovers to logos, attachments can form to a very wide and even bizarre range of things. As we'll see, decision makers can be affected by their attachments to cars and to the quality of a button-down shirt. The implication is that a wide range of potential attachments needs to be considered.

Attachments can be sunny or sinister in nature. We need to consider not just our positive attachments, but also "negative" attachments—such as An Wang's hostility toward IBM, described in chapter 3. Fear, hate, and regret can influence our decisions just as powerfully as can hope, love, and happy memories.

Attachments have subtle power. We often underestimate the effect of our own attachments, and those of others. Of all the emotions, those arising from attachments are most likely to seem benign. As a result, decision makers, and even those around them, are particularly prone to overlook the inherent dangers that attachments sometimes bring. The implication is that we need to be especially careful to think through the potential biases that may result from attachments.

An Astonishing Range of Attachments

The word *attachments* brings most readily to mind the social bonds that we form with family and friends. But as we'll see, we human beings can become attached to an extraordinary array of phenomena, including family and friends, communities and colleagues, and objects such as businesses, icons, or places.

Family and Friends

Love (or at least close connection) makes the world go round.

Even Adam Smith, famous as an icon for the view that self-interest is the critical force driving economies, believed social bonds to be a fundamental characteristic of being human: "How selfish soever man may be supposed, there are evidently some principles in his nature, which interest him in the fortune of others, and render their happiness necessary to him, though he derives nothing from it except the pleasure of seeing it."[24] Darwin, an icon for those who argue for the principle of the "survival of the fittest," similarly saw social relationships as fundamental to humanness: "Every one will admit that man is a social being. We see this in his dislike of solitude and in his wish for society beyond that of his own family. Solitary confinement is one of the severest punishments which can be inflicted."[25]

Intuitively, we know human beings to be social animals—we need social relationships, we will do things to develop and strengthen those relationships, and we grieve when those relationships are lost or broken.

In *Driven* Paul Lawrence and Nitin Nohria highlight explanations of why the "drive to bond," as they put it, is so fundamental.[26] The most basic type of bonding attachments are those to our spouses, family, friends, and the groups, societies, or organizations to which we belong. This can be explained partly through natural selection. Because early man lived in small groups, there were advantages to cooperating. Larger game could be hunted. It was easier to fight off enemies. Those individuals who helped their family and tribe did better than those who did not cooperate, because the whole tribe did better. Natural selection ensured that the genes that encouraged cooperative behavior were passed on through what is termed "reciprocal altruism."[27] A complementary explanation is that of sexual selection. Love, kindness, generosity, caring, and loyalty all evolved because women learned to appreciate them.[28] Only the men who exhibited these virtues got sex, had babies, and passed on their genes.[29] Today's women (and men) also find kindness attractive in a sexual partner—one study found it to be the most important attribute of partners in every one of the thirty-seven cultures surveyed.[30]

Communities and Colleagues

We also become attached to people other than close family. Just feeling that someone is like us or belongs to our group can cause us to form an attachment with them and influence our decision making.

For example, one of the exercises Sydney Finkelstein does at the Tuck School of Business at Dartmouth is a simulation of a negotiation that involves three parties. Each has different interests, and the exercise is designed to encourage conflict between and among the players. Any party can negotiate with any other; it is not necessary for all three to be involved in any negotiation. Sydney has run this exercise, with precisely the same rules, with two different groups at Tuck: resident MBA students, and senior executives who are attending a three-week training session. The results from the two groups have been consistently different. The MBA students typically negotiate the formation of a range of joint ventures that enable the parties to collaborate more than they compete. The executives, however, typically reach agreements that involve one or the other of the parties buying out their competitors.

Why this difference?

MBA students—especially those at a small school like Tuck that is known for its highly interactive and community-focused culture—become attached to each other during their two years together in ways that the executive education participants do not in just three weeks. For the Tuck MBA students, a negotiation agreement that allows each party to "save face" and play a role in the venture (even if such an agreement is not individually optimal) is a much more attractive option than it is for competitive executives who have not developed the same depth of attachment to their classmates. This pattern of results may also reflect differences in experience or other factors, but the role of interpersonal attachments seems front and center to understanding how these types of groups differ.

For an example of a more controlled experiment into how attachments can affect decision making, consider the following study. Participants were given a case in which a certain amount of money was split between themselves and a fictional partner (either a neighbor or a fellow student). The participants were given 126 different options of the total money available and the way the money was split and asked to score how happy they were about each option. However, there was a twist. Half of the participants were given a positive description of their partners implying that they felt attached to them—for example, that "you like the Smiths a lot." The other participants were given a very unfavorable description of their partners—for example, that "you have had many unpleasant personal experiences with the Smiths."

As you might expect, the participants were happier, all else being equal, when they received more money in absolute terms. They were also unhappy, all else being equal, when they received less than their partner—again, as one might expect. However, how they felt about receiving *more* than their partner proved particularly interesting.

Those participants who were given a very favorable description of their partners preferred that the Smiths receive the same as themselves and strongly disliked receiving more than them. For example, most participants, given a situation in which they were earning more than the Smiths, preferred to earn a hundred dollars less if that allowed the Smiths to earn a hundred dollars more. In other words, participants greatly valued that those they felt attached to were treated fairly and received an equal share to their own.

By contrast, the participants who were given a very unfavorable description of their partners tended to feel unconcerned or slightly happier if they received more than the Smiths.[31]

This study provides support for what we know instinctively to be true. Our decisions can be strongly influenced by how they will affect the people to whom we feel attached. We will feel negative emotions about options in which those we are attached to are treated in a way we view as unfair. We will feel positively about options that treat those we are attached to fairly. If our emotions then influence our judgment—perhaps because we are unaware of the full force of their influence—then they may inappropriately distort our decision making. Further—if participants in the experiment can be influenced by attachments generated by a written description of a hypothetical partner, how much more might our decision making be distorted if it affects those to whom we are really attached.

While attachments are generally laudable and certainly a part of our humanness, we need to recognize that they can affect our decision making—and can, in certain circumstances, lead to foolish decisions.

Beloved Objects

Things and places, just like people, can acquire particular significance—perhaps because of particularly strong emotional tags we associate with them from our previous experiences. For example, Lee Kun Hee, former chairman of Samsung, had an attachment to one of the more common objects people become attracted to: the motor car. However, in Lee's case, it contributed to a disastrous business decision.

Lee Kun Hee is the third son of Lee Byung Chull, who founded Samsung, the Korean electronics company. Lee Kun Hee went to university in Tokyo, went to business school in the United States, and managed different parts of the family company before, in 1987, he was named chairman.

When Lee Kun Hee took the reins, Samsung was riding high, with very profitable memory-chip and electronics businesses. On the back of this success, the new chief announced a "second founding" of the company and declared his intention to create a world-class corporation, ready for the twenty-first century. By 1995, he was close to achieving his goal. Samsung was among the top three companies in Korea and enjoyed a strong position in a range of industries that offered promise in the next century.

In that year, Lee Kun Hee made another dramatic announcement, one that puzzled many observers, as well as people within his own company: Samsung, Lee declared, would become an automaker. Yes, auto making was a growth industry, not only in Korea, but throughout Asia. Globally, however, the auto industry was mature. Automotive technology was advancing much more slowly than in the electronics segments, and world-class automakers were struggling with significant manufacturing overcapacity. Many questioned Lee's decision. As one Samsung insider explained, "Many believed that there were more and better investment opportunities and that the motor business was not a good choice at all."[32]

Chairman Lee Kun Hee also faced significant resistance from several outsiders. The Korean government had developed a policy that limited the number of companies that could participate in certain industries, to control competition and encourage a balanced economy. In general, the government wanted the large conglomerates to reduce the range of businesses they were involved in, not increase it. Korea already had two large automakers, Hyundai and Daewoo, so Samsung's request to enter the industry was denied by the Ministry of Trade, Industry, and Energy. The banks did not help Samsung's bid, either. They were reluctant to lend the huge sums required to create a plant that could produce enough units to be competitive—some 240,000. Because of the great risk involved, the banks insisted on guarantees from Samsung's other businesses.

Lee Kun Hee did not give up. He proposed locating the new factory in the home province of the president of Korea, Kim Young Sam, despite the cost disadvantage involved—nearly 40 percent more in setup costs per car than his competitors'. Samsung's engineers began to design their dream factory, a highly automated facility that contained internal roadways so wide (12 meters) that very large, automated vehicles could be employed in the facility and pass each other with plenty of room to spare. "The people at Samsung had no idea about the car business," says Kang Myung Han, former chief adviser at Samsung Motors. "Money was spent from the point of view of the engineer and spoiled executives, not the accountant."[33]

As Samsung continued to pursue the project, Samsung's Korean competitors tried to stop it. They discouraged their suppliers from producing parts for Samsung and refused to share know-how. As a result, Samsung had to establish relationships with untried suppliers in Korea and find new ones outside the country. Lee Kun Hee also agreed to license technology from Nissan, the Japanese carmaker, at a royalty of 1.7 percent of sales. Since the average return on sales made by Korean car companies was less than 2 percent, this Nissan royalty alone would have eaten up most of Samsung's profits—if they had made any at all. As Sydney Finkelstein concludes in his book *Why Smart Executives Fail*, "In the face of so many drawbacks, it would have taken a miracle for the car business to work."[34]

To make matters worse, the prospects for the car industry in Korea began to deteriorate, and sales growth slowed. The competitors were caught flat-footed, with expansion plans that would create nearly 1 million units of excess capacity. Analysts predicted that by 2000, capacity utilization might fall to just 60 percent. Even well-established and well-run carmakers, such as Nissan and Mazda, were finding the going tough.

Given all of these obstacles and bad omens, why did Chairman Lee continue to make flawed decisions in favor of moving ahead? There are many possible explanations. Possibly it was a case of his commitment making it impossible for him to recognize the evidence that this project would fail.

Most likely, however, it was an object attachment that confused the issue—Lee Kun Hee loved cars. It was no secret that Chairman Lee was a car enthusiast with a lifelong dream to build them himself. The press and other business leaders speculated that Lee's decision was driven partly by his passion for cars. As one internal manager commented, "Lee Kun Hee, chairman of Samsung Business Group, has been known by his love with cars. He just wanted to have a motor company in his portfolio of businesses."[35]

As almost everyone except Lee expected, the project turned into a disaster. In 1997, when the factory was partly built, the Asian economies went into a steep recession. Sales of cars in Korea and a number of other Asian countries collapsed. In the following twelve months, as industries and consumers struggled to reduce their high debt, car sales fell to less than 40 percent of their previous levels. In addition, large shifts in currency exchange rates led to sharp spikes in the cost of some imported parts.

Despite it all, Lee persisted, and Samsung's first cars rolled off the assembly line and were introduced to the market in March 1998. Despite rave reviews for the cars, Samsung Motors sold fewer than 50,000 units, many purchased by employees. In the first half of 1998, the motor division posted a net loss of 156 billion won, and debt for the Samsung Group rose to 3.6 trillion won. In December 1998, the main factory was closed, and in early 1999, Samsung Motors went into receivership.

The combination of the economic downturn of 1998 and 1999 and the failure of the motors division plunged Samsung Group into crisis. The labor force was reduced by 50,000, and Lee Kun Hee was compelled to pay some $2 billion from his personal fortune as part of the settlement with the creditors of the car business. In May 2000, the car-making operations were sold to Renault, the French automaker, for $120 million in cash and a further $440 million conditional on future profits—less than a tenth of Samsung's investment.

The range of objects we can become attached to is wide. One common attachment is to elements of the business that hold particular emotional significance for the decision maker. For example, the chairman of a large construction company visited an MBA class on corporate strategy taught by one of the authors. Prior to the class, a group of students had analyzed the various businesses of the company. They concluded that most of the businesses fit the competencies and skills of the company, which included procurement, project development, and large project management. However, one business stood out as a misfit: a provider of specialist advice for retailers seeking to refit their stores. This unit's main skills were in design and consultation with customers.

The chairman listened attentively as the group made its presentation, and then stood up to respond. After offering well-considered and detailed comments about the group's evaluation of the various businesses, he turned at last to the specialist retail business. "Yes," he said, "You're right. That business doesn't fit. But I like it! It's exciting. I enjoy it. Besides, it isn't too big a part of the business and doesn't absorb too much of my time—so I'm keeping it!"

An attachment was behind the chairman's decision to retain the design business. Perhaps it originated from his career prior to joining the construction company. He had spent his career working in relatively specialized and technologically sophisticated businesses. The construction company at which he now worked had businesses that were less technically advanced than he was used to, and less innovative and creative. He had developed a strong attachment to the innovative and creative style of the retail consultancy business, and that's why he told the MBA students that he would keep it in the company's portfolio even though it didn't really fit.

The implication is that some attachments can be particularly strong and thus particularly likely to influence a decision. Such passions may be hard to counter, appearing as visionary and inspirational to the decision maker and those around them.

Sunny or Sinister?

Chairman Lee's attachment to cars was highly positive (although it led to extremely negative results), but emotional tags can be negative as well. Hate, as well as love, can influence our decisions.

Negative feelings appear to have colored the decisions made by Craig Conway of PeopleSoft and Larry Ellison of Oracle during Ellison's takeover battle for PeopleSoft. As Conway himself put it, "This hostile tender offer would ultimately become one of the longest in history, taking almost 18 months and $200 million of legal fees by both companies."[36] Industry observers commented that both companies were damaged by the hostility of the process because they lost focus on customers and innovation, and rivals were able to pick up market share.

The battle was rough and got very nasty at times. Ellison at first vowed that he would gut PeopleSoft, lay off the majority of its staff, phase out its products, and destroy customer confidence in the company. Later, Oracle reassured the world that it would support PeopleSoft products for at least the next ten years. PeopleSoft was as vicious as Ellison was unpredictable. Conway created a fiendishly clever "poison pill" strategy to keep the Oracle marauders at bay: PeopleSoft promised to pay its customers a rebate equal to two to five times the amount of their annual contract fees if PeopleSoft were taken over.

What made this particular takeover battle so vitriolic? Larry Ellison and Craig Conway hated each other. Ellison is famous for the size of his ego and his dominating personality. Many of his lieutenants could not tolerate Ellison's style and quit Oracle to work for rival companies, and one of the most notable of these was Craig Conway. Ellison never forgave him. "At one point Craig thought I was going to shoot his dog," Ellison said. "I love animals. If Craig and the dog were standing next to each other, trust me—if I had one bullet—it wouldn't be for the dog."[37] Finally, the PeopleSoft board sacked Conway, and the deal was done.

We can have hostile feelings about others because of some previous event (as in the case of Ellison and Conway) or simply because they belong to a rival group.[38] Sometimes such hostility is disguised as loyalty to our own group, as in the case of gang members who will attack rival gangs just because they are different. In the United Kingdom, for example, some gang members associate with one another because they live within the same postcode (zip code) and attack rival gangs because they are from a different one. For example, in April 2007, a London boy was stabbed to death by a rival gang. One local resident explained the cause of the attack: "The Thatched House boys are E15 and the Cathall Boys are E11: it's all about postcodes."[39] Researchers have conducted experiments confirming that we can act in a parochial fashion, being prepared to sacrifice our own interests for the interests of our group while at the same time being aware that our group is benefiting only at the expense of others.[40] We are particularly hostile to people we regard as "traitors": those who are members of the group but take actions that are against the group's interests.

Negative feelings may influence our decisions in a similar but opposite way to positive feelings of attachment. For example, envy counteracts our desire for fairness and helping others, and can affect our decisions by making us choose options that allow us to gain an advantage over others. Fear can lead us to take preemptive action against others to stop them from getting ahead or harming us. Both have been shown to have an influence on our decisions in laboratory experiments.[41] These experiments also suggest that such feelings are more likely to affect our decisions when we do not trust others—for example, when they are not known to us. In the context of strategic decisions, we are more likely to be affected by hostile feelings if we distrust the actions of others involved in the decision.

The existence of negative feelings has an important implication for identifying red flags. Decisions may be influenced not only by positive emotional attachments, but also by feelings of hostility, aversion, envy, or fear. It is important to ask not only, "What attachments does the decision maker have?" but also, "What hostile feelings might affect his or her judgment?"

Attachments Beguile Us

Like any emotion, the effect of emotions generated by our attachments can be extremely beguiling, so beguiling, in fact, that they can be very hard to spot. Even if we are aware of the feelings they create, we may be unaware of how they are affecting our decision. However, attachments also have certain additional features that make it even more likely that we underestimate their impact. In particular, attachments often act under disguise. They invoke a feeling that we are being objectively rational when, in fact, we are being swayed by potentially inappropriate feelings.

For example, Andrew realized *later* that his attachment to his original logo was irrational. At the time, although he was aware of the power of his feelings, he also believed his arguments to be reasonable. He felt intuitively that the existing logo was important, and he searched for arguments that supported retaining it. Why, if he was aware of the strength of his feelings, was he unable to recognize and counteract the bias it might be causing? Why did he allow his reasoning mind (he is extremely good at arguing a point) to become hijacked by his feelings? Part of the reason is that attachments create intuitive arguments that are particularly seductive. If our attachments are for others, then arguing on their behalf appears altruistic. If the attachment is to a symbol of something good—in Andrew's case, the development from scratch of a research center—then arguing on its behalf also feels good.

In chapter 6, we talked about Steve Russell, chief executive of Boots, and his decision to enter health-care services. Part of his explicit argument in favor of this particular growth strategy was that the Boots employees needed something important to believe in. His attachment to employees certainly must have seemed to him and others as a reasonable and laudable reason to search for new opportunities for what had become a large but stagnating base business. But it contributed to a flawed decision to venture into health-care services.

Consider also the example of Marks & Spencer's flawed acquisition of Brooks Brothers, the clothier. In 1988 Marks & Spencer (M&S), led by its chairman, Derek Rayner, acquired Brooks Brothers for $750 million. Brooks Brothers, a retail chain famous for its button-down shirts, represented the clothing tradition of Wall Street and American business. Rayner wanted the company because he felt it would provide a foundation on which M&S could build a successful business in the United States. But as it turned out, he had purchased a turkey. The day the deal was announced, M&S shares fell 4p, to 180p, despite the respect with which M&S was held. Brooks Brothers never performed successfully, and when M&S finally sold it for $225 million in November 2001, it had cost the company more than $1 billion.

Why did Rayner make such a mistake?

After all, he knew that retailing skills don't always travel well. M&S's earlier experience in North America had proved this. The previous chairman, Marcus Sieff, had acquired Peoples Department Stores in Canada, and it had proved to be his greatest mistake. As described in Judi Bevan's *The Rise and Fall of Marks & Spencer*, M&S's format simply did not suit the Canadian shopper. "When one Alberta woman was asked why she did not shop at her local Marks & Spencer, she replied that she had no wish to shop in a hospital ward."[42] Rayner was, therefore, well aware that M&S's success in the U.K. might not translate into overseas markets.

Rayner also had a good idea of Brooks Brothers' market value, which his team that was working on the acquisition put at about $450 million, rather than the $750 million he eventually paid. Rayner's team also suggested an alternative acquisition—but Rayner rejected that option and stuck with Brooks Brothers.[43] What's more, Rayner was highly intelligent and had a strong performance record. In the four years of his leadership, 1984–1988, M&S had modernized, transformed itself from a family-run company, doubled earnings per share, and grown revenues from £2.9 to £4.6 billion.

Given all his knowledge and experience, what caused Rayner to pay almost double the market value for Brooks Brothers?

The reason: Rayner loved the product. He "was enamored with Brooks Brothers clothing, which was in large part aimed at men of Rayner's age and taste." Although his advisers had presented six possible acquisition targets, Rayner ignored all the others and "went straight for the preppy upmarket Brooks Brothers chain."[44]

Rayner's attachment to Brooks Brothers and its products is not so surprising in light of his personal history. He had been with M&S for more than thirty years when he became chairman, almost all of which had been spent under the wing of Marcus Sieff, the previous chairman. Sieff, and the other members of the family who had led the company for a century, had created a culture in which the quality of product and suppliers was paramount—as was the quality of the lifestyle enjoyed by the company's directors, who all tooled about in chauffeur-driven Rolls-Royce cars and convened their executive meetings at only the most luxurious hotels.

Rayner had steeped himself in quality and focused on minute details. "Every morning at 7:30," writes Bevan, "the top food executives would meet on the sixth floor in an area known as the Bureau of Standards and taste samples of all the new season fruit that had been delivered that day. 'There was always an issue,' said Stuart Rose, then a food executive and now the company's executive chairman. 'The nectarines were too sharp or the melon not ripe. Derek was obsessive. I remember falling out with him over the quality of the mangoes.'[45]

Rayner had an unshakable attachment to quality, and the Brooks Brothers name was synonymous with quality. Not only were its button-down shirts and natural-shoulder suits a legendary uniform on Wall Street; its stores offered unhurried, old-fashioned, and courteous service. Rayner was told by the sellers that Brooks Brothers was a trophy prize that merited a trophy price—and he swallowed the rationale whole.

What may have made his attachment to Brooks Brothers so beguiling was that Rayner could have justified the acquisition with the argument that a quality company with a quality product would surely be a good fit with Marks & Spencer. This would have made it almost impossible for him to appreciate the extent to which he was being influenced by emotional attachments of which he was only partly conscious, and difficult for him to see why Brooks Brothers was worth only half of what he paid.

As with most real-life decisions, there were other red flag conditions that almost certainly also played a role; but the thing that seems to set Rayner apart from his M&S colleagues—who urged caution—was his attachment to the Brooks Brothers product and service.

What all these cases have in common is that the arguments generated by the decision makers likely felt quite reasonable. Andrew Campbell felt that his logo suited his organization better than the new, corporate one. Steve Russell wanted to give hope to the Boots organization. Derek Rayner felt that buying a company that was the byword for quality fit his vision for M&S.

Attachments Feel Good

Attachments can not only feel reasonable; they can often drive us to make decisions that generate good feelings—adding to the risk that they beguile and deceive us. For example, decisions that threaten people or things we are attached to can produce powerful feelings of guilt and strong protective feelings that strongly influence our choices. These feelings seem reasonable but can lead us to make flawed decisions.

The personal assistant (PA) of one of the authors was fired, on the spot, by the office manager when she discovered that the PA had accessed and read a private e-mail of a colleague. The author argued forcefully that the procedure followed was inappropriate and a more measured process should have been used. He argued that doing so might have highlighted some of the extenuating circumstances that led to the PA's transgression.

Sometime after this event, however, the author realized that the real reason for his objection to the firing was his attachment to his PA, because they had worked closely together over a period of several years. While this attachment was not unusual, it was surprising (to the author, at least) that he had not been aware at the time of the firing how much this attachment was driving his actions. He felt guilt and shame at the actions of the company and strongly protective of his assistant, who was suddenly out of a job. His feelings were accentuated by his dislike (negative attachment) of the office manager, whom he resented and felt to be imperious and cold—although later on he realized that she was only trying to be consistent and disciplined.

Unlike the Wolfowitz case, this was not about romantic love—but, like love, it released a complex and powerful cocktail of feelings: guilt, shame, resentment, tenderness, and caring. The author was partly aware of these feelings but not fully aware of the distorting effect they were having on his arguments.

Attachments can tap into strong emotions, with dramatic consequences for the quality of our decisions. The implication: don't underestimate their effect.

Identifying Inappropriate Attachments

We describe here how to identify attachments that may be inappropriate for the decision being considered. We do this relatively briefly because the process is similar to that for identifying inappropriate self-interest.

From experience, the following are the most common sources of attachments:

- **People working with the decision maker.** CEOs may feel attachments to the managers who are submitting plans for approval. Managers may feel attachments to direct reports who are applying for a more senior position. Indeed, it would be disturbing to find a business leader who didn't develop attachments to some of the people they worked with.

- **People with nonwork affiliations to the decision maker.** For example, in the decision exercise at Tuck Business School described earlier, MBA students, who were together on campus for many months, made different decisions from executives, who only came together for a few days. The students had clearly developed attachments that influenced their choices.

- **Elements of the business.** Decision makers develop attachments to business units, factories, work sites, functions, and processes in much the same way that the chairman of the construction company developed an attachment to the retail consultancy business. Decision makers can also form strong associations with suppliers, distributors, and customer groups. For example, the leaders of Marks & Spencer became attached to the company's local suppliers. There were personal relationships with the leaders of many of the supplier companies. It took a collapse in M&S's profits and the appointment of a new chairman to initiate a significant shift toward international sourcing.

  Attachments can also be negative. An Wang hated IBM. This attachment contributed to his bad decision regarding the operating system of the Wang personal computer.

- **Iconic things.** Logos, products, gifts, mementos—almost any object can become a symbol to a decision maker. For Rayner, the

Brooks Brothers shirt was a symbol of quality that appealed to him—the product was targeted at people of his age in the corporate world. Andrew was greatly attached to the original logo of Ashridge, which symbolized for him the organization that he had helped to found and develop.

- **Places.** Places where the decision maker worked, spent key periods of time, or had a particularly formative experience can lead to remarkably powerful attachments. Anyone who has ever tried to entice someone to relocate for a promising new opportunity, and has come up against a brick wall understands just how powerful such attachments can be.

Given this wide range of possible attachments and given the difficulty of knowing about all the attachments an individual has, we need some practical way of analyzing attachments so that we can identify any that may be inappropriate. As with self-interest, we need to identify those that might significantly influence the decision and whose influence is at odds with the interests of other stakeholders. We therefore suggest the following questions to ask when trying to spot inappropriate attachments:

1. Do any of the options affect people, places, or things to which the decision maker is likely to be attached or hostile?

2. Are these attachments likely to conflict with the interests of the main stakeholders?

3. Are any conflicting attachments likely to be strong enough to significantly distort the decision?

As an example, consider An Wang, whom we discussed earlier in this book. He faced the choice of whether or not to produce a personal computer compatible with the IBM PC. Wang had two attachments affecting this decision: his attachment to the Wang word processor, a product which would be partly replaced by a PC, and his deep hostility to IBM. Do these attachments conflict with the interests of the main stakeholders—

his shareholders? Yes they do. Are they likely to be strong enough to distort the decision? Yes they are, and, as far as we understand, An Wang's decision making was distorted by these attachments, causing him to make a major mistake.

Or, consider Derek Rayner, who faced the decision of whether or not to acquire Brooks Brothers. He had an important attachment—the Brooks Brothers' button-down shirt, or at least the quality image that this shirt symbolized. If those around him had been asked what sort of company Rayner would most like, Brooks Brothers would have been an obvious choice. Was this attachment in conflict with the interests of his stakeholders? Not necessarily. Potentially this attachment could have helped Rayner find good acquisition targets. On the other hand, it is only one criterion to be considered. Potentially, Rayner's thinking could be unbalanced by his love of quality. Might this possible conflict cause him to make the wrong decision? Yes, it could. Clearly Rayner's attachment to the button-down shirt is a red flag condition. What is more it appeared to influence his thinking. He immediately selected Brooks Brothers from a list of six possible targets, and was willing to pay well above the price his team advised. Again the result was a bad decision.

In summary, inappropriate attachments can be spotted in advance. However, they can also be among the most difficult causes of flawed decisions to anticipate. They are so entwined in the daily lives of decision makers that they can be difficult to spot without intimate knowledge of the people concerned. Also, most of the time they are seen as positive, at least by the decision maker. Our attachments to family and friends, communities, beloved objects, and our own past are part of our identity, not something to be ashamed of. Hence, exposing them as possible red flags can be awkward. Nevertheless, they account at least in part for over 40 percent of decision errors.

In this chapter, we have pointed out many of the ways in which attachments can lead us astray, and we have explained why it is possible to be influenced by our attachments even when we are trying not to be. We have also described how to identify the red flag conditions when our attachments are inappropriate and might significantly distort our decision. In part 3, we turn to the issue of how to protect decisions from the risk of distortion.

PART THREE

Red Flags and Safeguards

NINE

Reducing Risks
with Safeguards

N O ONE IS IMMUNE. Think back to when John F. Kennedy became U.S. president in January 1961. One of the first decisions he faced was a plan to overthrow Fidel Castro's new Marxist regime in Cuba. The plan, developed by the CIA under Kennedy's predecessor, President Eisenhower, called for an invasion by Cuban exiles, with U.S. military support, including air cover and drops by paratroopers to secure the approaches to the landing beaches. The invasion forces were meant to join up with other Cubans opposed to Castro, who had a stronghold in the mountains behind the planned invasion site.

Kennedy was less hostile to Castro than Eisenhower had been. He recognized that the regime Castro had overthrown was corrupt. But he allowed the plan to go ahead with two alterations: he wanted the operation to be undertaken entirely by Cubans, so that U.S. involvement was "deniable"; and he insisted that the landing take place at night in an area with little opposition. The only option was the Bay of Pigs.

The operation was launched in April 1961. It was a disaster. The plan had been leaked. The Bay of Pigs was miles from rebel strongholds on the island, and Castro's forces quickly closed in, preventing the invaders from leaving the beaches. Despite some air strikes, the lack of U.S. military support allowed the Cuban army to overcome the invaders and kill or capture all of them within three days. Kennedy was forced to negotiate for the release of the survivors. It was a military catastrophe and a political setback. In hindsight, it was clear that even if the plan had not been leaked, the chances of success had been minimal. The decision to invade was flawed.

What went wrong? The list is long. Kennedy's plan was based on his prejudgment that visible U.S. involvement was unacceptable. His changes, made for political reasons and without the advice of his generals, condemned the operation militarily.

In addition to his prejudgments, there was an element of self-interest in his decision to go ahead with the plan. While he had personal misgivings about the whole enterprise, Kennedy was under domestic political pressure to do something about Cuba and was accused by opponents of being weak.

Kennedy's prejudgments and self-interest might not have been a problem if his decision process had included some safeguards. Unfortunately, he talked almost exclusively to the CIA and failed to consult more broadly. As his national security adviser, McGeorge Bundy, remarked, Kennedy "made up his mind and did not tell us."[1]

Learning from Disaster

The Bay of Pigs was a military and political fiasco. But Kennedy learned from his mistake. When, on October 16, 1962, Bundy told him that the Russians had placed intermediate-range nuclear missiles in Cuba, Kennedy recognized that it would be easy to prejudge the situation, draw on misleading experiences, or be over-influenced by self-interest.

Powerful but misleading experiences were often invoked during the debate about what to do. Pearl Harbor was mentioned frequently, the implication being that it was a sneak attack, the opening move in a war. So was Munich—which implied that the United States should on no account appease an expansionist regime but must stand up to aggression.

The inference drawn was that the United States should respond militarily, as if it were already at war. Kennedy initially shared this view—telling a close adviser, "I suppose the alternatives are to go in by air and wipe them out, or to take other steps to render the weapons inoperable."[2]

Actually, both Pearl Harbor and Munich were misleading analogies: they occurred at a time when neither side had nuclear weapons. Because both the United States and Russia now had a nuclear arsenal, responding militarily involved taking a huge risk that the world would be enveloped by a nuclear holocaust. To counterbalance the effects of these potential red flags, Kennedy set up a decision process to create room for rigorous and multifaceted debate. The ExComm committee included members of all the relevant government agencies, trusted personal advisers, and some older hands to add to the depth and range of experience. This ensured that a wide range of options would be considered, assessed, and debated from various perspectives. Among the fifteen members of ExComm were supporters of aggressive military action, including the current and former secretaries of state, Dean Rusk and Dean Acheson; CIA director John McCone; and chairman of the Joint Chiefs of Staff General Maxwell Taylor. There were also people who were strongly opposed to an air strike, such as the secretary of defense, Robert McNamara, and Kennedy's friend and special counsel Theodore Sorensen. Added to the mix for some meetings were people such as Adlai Stevenson, U.S. ambassador to the UN, who contributed input on the diplomatic options.[3]

To ensure that these different perspectives were used to create a healthy debate, Kennedy insisted that ExComm work until its members reached consensus. This forced them to debate in depth. He knew that total agreement would be impossible but, by demanding consensus, he ensured that everyone would at least be prepared to go along with the preferred option, and do their best to make it work. To ensure that all focused on the nuclear risk, a sign was placed outside the main briefing room during the crisis. It read, "In a Nuclear Age, nations must make war like porcupines make love—carefully."[4]

Rather than chair the committee himself, he asked his brother Robert Kennedy to lead the decision-making process. This limited the chance that the president would become anchored on one of the options. But, he retained a strong influence over the decision and the decision process by intervening at key moments. For example, President Kennedy rejected early options involving air strikes or invasion, asking ExComm to think again to see whether there was a solution that reduced the risks of nuclear war. As a result, they came up with what proved to be the best option: a blockade of Cuba. The president's own role during this decision was one of governance, of rejecting unacceptable options and pressing for more until resolution was reached.

He then closely monitored how the blockade was conducted, seeking both to stand firm and to offer conciliation. He directed McNamara to ensure that the navy and the air force did not inadvertently undermine his strategy. He used the time gained by the blockade to send signals to Soviet Premier Khrushchev. Finally, Kennedy found a way of allowing Khrushchev to back down without losing face, by using backdoor Russian contacts to secure a trade: the withdrawal of U.S. missiles stationed in Turkey for Soviet agreement to dismantle the missiles in Cuba.

Safer with Safeguards

Kennedy recognized the red flag conditions and created a process that reduced the risk of a flawed decision. The process addressed the specific red flag conditions by selecting what we call *safeguards*.

Safeguards can involve a wide range of interventions, process changes, people choices, analytical techniques, and other mechanisms that can be put in place to reduce the risk of a flawed decision. While every organization has some sort of process to manage decisions, we define safeguards as *additional* measures, chosen because they are appropriate to a particular decision. We use this term because they provide a guard against flawed decisions, although not a guarantee that no mistakes will be made. We cannot eliminate human biases, but we can counterbalance their potential effects.

Our research uncovered four different categories of safeguard.

1. *Experience, Data, and Analysis*

One type of safeguard is to provide decision makers with new experiences or data and analysis. By doing so, the risk of a flawed decision can be reduced at the source. In the case of the Cuban Missile Crisis, Kennedy needed to know the number, location, and state of readiness of the missiles—so that he could better judge whether it was feasible to carry out a military strike and the time he had available before the Soviets would have a functioning and significant threat to U.S. security. So he had the air force carry out reconnaissance flights.

In business, there are many ways data can be collected and experience broadened. A discussion with a key customer can provide valuable feedback on a proposed new product. Market research might evaluate the risks of entering a new market. Consultants could be brought in, partly for their expertise and readily available manpower, but also because they are relatively objective. BP sometimes employs two firms of lawyers to get contrasting views for very important decisions, such as major acquisitions.

Sometimes the sources of new experience and data go beyond the obvious. For example, Jack Welch decided that GE's businesses needed to move quickly to take advantage of the opportunities offered by the Internet. But how could he get a bunch of traditional GE managers to make decisions about Internet investments, when most of them knew next to nothing about it? (Welch confessed, "I was afraid of [the Internet], because I couldn't type.") Part of his answer was to expose them to new experiences and data by directing the top six hundred managers to find an internal "Internet mentor," typically a younger colleague who tutored them in Web behavior. His intention was to expose them to the power of the Internet and give them firsthand experience of what it could do. Welch had his own transforming experience of the power of the Internet when he watched his family and colleagues do their Christmas shopping online![5]

Sometimes new data is not what is required. Even if there is time to collect new information, decision makers are often too entrenched in their current views to be shifted by new data alone. They may have previous experiences or judgments that stimulate strong emotions making it hard for them to absorb or react to new data. Or they may have personal interests and attachments that continue to distort their thinking even when they are presented with new inputs. Military men see military solutions. New data or experiences are unlikely to remove this bias.

In these cases, something more is needed. One approach is to create a challenging debate.

2. Group Debate and Challenge

Creating a debate which challenges biases need not involve an elaborate process. It could mean simply chatting through an issue with a friend or colleague. Even if the other person is not an expert, the process of debate can help expose assumptions and beliefs. In large organizations a typical way to orchestrate debate and challenge is to form a decision group. The size of the team may vary from two to many, although typically a few people are a better number for a debate.

The choice of who should be on the team is vital in defining the quality of challenge that can take place. For example, a U.K. food company with several business divisions sometimes chooses a manager from a sister division to chair the decision group. The intention is to bring a challenging, and potentially more objective, perspective to the decision. Kennedy's ExComm was chosen to include diverse views.

The ability of a group to debate effectively is driven not only by its composition, but by the process it follows. Many choices can be made about the process—such as whether to use an independent facilitator; whether to set up subgroups to evaluate different parts of the decision or to take different perspectives; how much time to take; how many meetings to have; what to discuss; and so on. For example, ExComm was required to come to a consensus decision—forcing members to debate intensely. In one company, the CEO was concerned that his managers appeared to be anchored to the status quo. So he started the planning process by asking each manager to compose an imaginary article to appear in the *Financial Times* in ten years' time, describing the achievements of the current management team over the "past" ten years. The goal was to get each individual to generate creative ideas of how the business might be developed, and so provide a good platform for a debate over a wide range of options. After the exercise, one member of the management team commented that the new plan was "the first time we have had a real strategy."

Processes that challenge entrenched views are a critical source of safeguards. Strong leaders need a strong challenge. If, as is often the case, the affected decision maker cannot or will not be removed from the decision process, there are a range of tools and approaches to provide an "extreme challenge." Some are very simple, such as conducting private one-on-one interviews to identify different viewpoints and then playing back the range of views to the decision makers; pairing up a decision maker with a senior individual with different experiences and viewpoints; or having a session to brainstorm different frames, options, or criteria. Other more elaborate approaches involve creating different roles in the decision process, such as splitting the authorizer, evaluator, and proposer roles; using the "RAPID" approach (allocating decision responsibilities, such as recommend, agree, perform, input, decide, to different people); or allocating "hats" to different people (as suggested by the lateral thinker, Edward de Bono).[6] There are also highly structured approaches, such as creating customized role-plays; using red teams; dialectical inquiry (asking a separate group to present an alternative option and then having the whole group work together to identify the best option); or the devil's advocate method (in which a subgroup attacks the proposed option).[7]

Finally, we would like to highlight one other way to challenge the decision makers: reframing the decision. We have seen this in our own teaching and consulting. Groups that spend time at the beginning of a decision identifying alternative frames for the decision are more likely to challenge their own thinking. Even more powerful is to spend time reframing the decision at some point *during* the process. This helps decision makers to take on board emerging facts and insights. This new data can easily be overlooked if the decision makers have become anchored on a particular way of looking at the situation.

For example, in a popular executive course, we run an exercise in which the participants tend initially to frame the issue as "How can we use a new technology to improve our position in the market?" But as they analyze the numbers, they find that the financial returns on investing are highly negative (the technology is capital intensive and cannibalizes existing profitable product lines). Undaunted, they frequently go through incredible contortions of their logic to find ways to justify investment (particularly those assigned to play the role of the marketing department). Typically, groups only begin to make progress when they reframe the decision as "How do we avoid a competitive arms race in which all competitors spend a lot of money investing in this new technology?" or "How do we keep things as they are?" They then start thinking about options such as patenting technology or signaling to competitors.

What if debate is not enough? In some situations genuine debate is difficult to generate—or unlikely to affect the views of the primary decision maker. For example, when there is a powerful, charismatic, and (up to that point) successful decision maker, challenging him or her to think again may simply be impractical. We have already seen how Sir Clive Thompson pushed through a couple of large acquisitions that did not fit the capabilities of the company, Rentokil, of which he was the chief executive. Steve Russell, CEO of Boots, led the company into a flawed health-care services strategy. Challenging such individuals by redesigning the decision group and process is unlikely to be effective—especially when the individuals concerned are in charge of the design. In such situations, an even stronger safeguard is required. Sometimes the only way to significantly reduce the risk of a flawed decision is through a strong governance process. This is the third type of safeguard.

3. Governance

The governance team approves the proposal submitted by the decision team. President Kennedy gave himself this role in the Cuban Missile

Crisis. In the case of a major acquisition, the decision team might be the CEO and the CFO, and the governance team might be the board led by the chairman. In the case of a corporatewide reorganization, the decision team might be a task force consisting of the heads of a couple of the business units, led by the head of human resources, and the governance team might be the full executive committee led by the CEO. Sometimes there is no separate governance team. In these cases it may be necessary to set one up.

The governance team is a vital backstop—designed to stand in the way of any flawed judgments that make it past the decision team. Few large organizations allow the decision proposer to also authorize important decisions. Often there are independent, non–executive board members or trustees to increase the objectivity of the authorization process.

In the course of writing this book, we have become much more respectful of governance processes and the value of independent chairmen. Prior to this research, we were skeptical about the amount of effort being put into corporate governance and the need to have independent chairmen of public companies. We felt that independent chairmen are unlikely to understand the businesses well; hence they may be more of a hindrance than a help. However, having completed this research, we are more aware of the problem that independent chairmen can solve: helping protect against flawed decisions.[8]

This is true, of course, at all levels in the organization. When any important decision is being made, it is useful to think about governance. Who is remaining independent from this decision so that he or she can be objective enough to say no if the team comes up with a flawed proposal?

As we write, debate is raging about the governance of Marks & Spencer, the iconic British retailer. In March 2008, M&S announced that it was making its "charismatic and autocratic" CEO, Sir Stuart Rose, executive chairman—combining the roles of CEO and chairman.[9] The previous chairman, Lord Burns, said it "was important to retain Stuart Rose in the business for longer . . . We want him to play a bigger role in terms of developing the next generation of leaders so that by the time he leaves we have a new chief executive in place. This reduces the uncertainty over whether he will stay or not."[10]

The announcement was met with fury from major investors.[11] Many of their stated concerns were about the resulting concentration of power and the lack of an independent voice and debating partner should Rose make a flawed judgment. With M&S unwilling to change its decision to appoint Stuart Rose as chairman, discussions with shareholders then centered on how to strengthen the board: to make it strong enough to resist Stuart Rose, if he were to make a flawed judgment.[12] Rose argued that Sir David Michels, the senior non-executive could play this role. He had given up two other directorships to spend more time on M&S business. But, most observers were skeptical. In the words of one CEO and chairman, "If you've got a CEO who is also a chairman, there is no focal point for the independent directors. With a group of equals, sometimes no director is willing to say 'I think this CEO or this idea is out of line.' The directors wait until things get so bad that firing the CEO is the only way to rectify the problems."[13]

When red flags exist that cannot be addressed by additional data or additional debate an independent chairman is vital. Any company that abandons this option, as M&S has, is rejecting a powerful safeguard against bad decisions.

As with the decision group, it is not only the membership of a governance layer that is important. The process that they use to address the decision is also important. Governance levels can hire independent advisors, demand analysis of overlooked options, require inputs at different stages of the decision process, and more. There are many process tools that can strengthen the governance of a decision. For example, aware of the ease with which managers can become attached to acquisition targets, boards often have well established processes to help them defend against this red flag condition. It is common for managers to be required to bring the acquisition proposal to the board on three occasions: to alert the board that managers are considering a target; to get the board's approval to indicate a price range for the business; and to approve the final terms. The sequence of interactions gives the governance level plenty of warning of the deal and multiple opportunities to assess the objectivity of the managers involved.

Sometimes, however, even the governance process is not sufficiently powerful. Perhaps the governance team does not have the expertise required. Or perhaps the governance team is not powerful enough to provide sufficient challenge. Strong business leaders, for example, have often been involved in appointing the members of their boards.

Another potential problem is that the governance group may have its own biases. Consider the case of Marconi, a British electronics company that spectacularly imploded in the wake of the 2001 crash of technology stocks. In February 2000, the deputy chief executive, John Mayo, recommended to the board that it sell or merge the company. He felt the company was too small to survive on its own in the rapidly consolidating telecoms market. As Mayo reported, the board of Marconi was biased by recent successes: the company had been able to grow rapidly, generating exceptional returns for shareholders. He quotes one independent director as saying, "We didn't give up on the beaches of Dunkirk, and we are not going to give up now." According to Mayo, "No other main board director was prepared to support the proposal (to sell the company) and consequently the board rejected it."[14] A few months later the company was in freefall.

In these situations, the last line of defense is to increase the monitoring of the early progress of the decision, with the aim of changing course if things do not turn out as planned. This is the fourth type of safeguard.

4. Monitoring

The monitoring process tracks the progress of the decision. Awareness that this will happen can encourage decision makers to think carefully before making their recommendations. If decision makers know that the outcome will be recorded and publicized, this can be enough to cause them to "think again."

Monitoring can also help to modify a wrong decision quickly—for example, a growth investment may be curtailed if early performance is disappointing. In some cases, the monitoring process is a standard part of the decision process—as in test marketing by consumer goods or retail companies, which monitor the rollout of products and adjust their plans according to the results. In other cases a specially designed monitoring process can be installed for a specific decision.

Monitoring, of course, is a normal part of almost every decision. What we are suggesting here is that, for some decisions, where there are red flag conditions that managers believe are hard to address with the first three categories of safeguard, then the last defense is to put in place some extra monitoring. The safeguard is the extra monitoring over and above what would have occurred anyway.

Extra monitoring is the final backstop: the last safeguard against a bad decision. It is particularly useful when no other alternative appears to offer protection. In the case of the Cuban Missile Crisis, Kennedy could not be sure that he had made the right decision. He knew he had limited data about how the Russians would respond to his decision to blockade Cuba. As a result, he opened extra channels of communication with Khrushchev to monitor the impact of the blockade on his thinking. This gave Kennedy more information about the Russian leader's reactions and helped him come up with the idea of trading the missiles in Turkey for those in Cuba.

For a business example, consider the case of the flawed health-care services strategy at Boots. Because of the unusual circumstances (the previous CEO was now chairman and was reluctant to overrule the new CEO), it was hard for the Board to block the strategy. But, the board could have demanded extra monitoring, such as frequent reporting of performance to a special board subcommittee. As it turns out, information about early problems was not elevated to senior levels until it was too late. Monitoring took place—but was not well enough designed to be an effective safeguard.

We believe that it is possible to design some form of safeguard for almost any situation where red flags exist. Of course, we cannot protect all decisions. But careful thought about safeguards can dramatically reduce the number of bad decisions.

A counter argument is that most large organizations already have structured decision processes with built in safeguards. These exist because of past mistakes. In other words, most leaders already recognize the need for good process to reduce the risk of flawed decisions. So are we offering anything new? The answer is yes. We are suggesting that decision processes need to be tailored to the red flags that might distort the decision. The elaborate processes that are part of the standard way of making decisons often generate a bureaucratic environment that breeds disrespect for the process. In our view, the standard process should be light, reducing cost and building respect. Safeguards should then be added to the process as needed for particular decisions.

The Iraq Decision

Kennedy learned from the Bay of Pigs experience and introduced safeguards to guide his decision making over the Cuban Missile Crisis. Interestingly, it was his earlier mistakes that helped him recognize the red flags. More recently, Tony Blair, the British prime minister, did not have the benefit of a mistake, like the Bay of Pigs, to help him realize the importance of safeguards when deciding whether to go to war in Iraq.

Prior to the Iraq decision, Tony Blair had three relevant but potentially misleading experiences: in the Balkans, in Sierra Leone, and in Afghanistan. In all three cases, military intervention or a credible threat of military intervention succeeded or appeared to succeed in resolving the situation.

For example, Tony Blair personally persuaded a reluctant President Clinton to threaten the Serbian leader, Milosevic, with military invasion if he did not back down over Kosovo. The threat worked. Milosevic backed down and was then overthrown in an internal political coup. The policy of making a credible threat of military intervention worked.

These earlier experiences encouraged Blair to support military intervention in Iraq. With hindsight, this appears to have been misleading. Blair was certainly more enthusiastic than the British foreign secretary or the chancellor of the exchequer, neither of whom had such personal involvement in these earlier events.

Of course, these experiences might not have been misleading. They only turned out to be misleading because the situation in Iraq was different in some important ways. Most prominently, Iraq was a fractured society which had only been held together by brutal force.

In 2001, prior to 9/11, Tony Blair argued that the powerful nations could make the world a better place if they intervened in failing states or confronted unsavory dictators. When considering what to do about Iraq, he probably tagged the intervention plan with a strong positive emotion because it reinforced his prejudgment about the benefits of intervention.

Again, Blair's prejudgment in favor of intervention might not have been misleading. But it is likely to have influenced his thinking, making him more enthusiastic about intervention than was probably appropriate. He was certainly more enthusiastic than his opposite numbers in France, Germany, and Russia, none of whom had made a similar prejudgment.

Tony Blair's interventionist policy made him popular with George Bush following 9/11. It put him center stage. Some people even referred to him as "deputy leader of the world." In this context, an interventionist policy in Iraq may have seemed more personally attractive than a wait-and-see policy. Unconsciously, the interventionist plan may have attracted more positive emotions because of his personal interests.

When it became clear that the United States was willing to invade Iraq with or without British support, Blair's attachment to Bush and to the longstanding "special relationship" between the two nations may have made him more enthusiastic about supporting the venture than he should have been. He was certainly more enthusiastic than the 1 million people (2 percent of the population) who marched in London to try to persuade him not to back the invasion.

Stepping back and with the benefit of hindsight, it is clear that there were red flags in all four categories. Of course, we do not know for sure whether Tony Blair's thinking was affected by these experiences, prejudgments, interests, and attachments, but it seems probable that it was, and it seems likely that these influences affected his judgment.

Unfortunately, like Kennedy's Bay of Pigs decision, Blair did not put in place safeguards that could have challenged his point of view or given it less weight in the final call. For example, although the topic was discussed a number of times in Cabinet, there does not appear to have been a decision point or a vote. As a close observer commented, "Blair did not use Cabinet in that way."

What safeguards might have challenged Tony Blair's thinking? First, he could have pushed for more consideration of the data he was getting from the intelligence services. With the same data coming from his intelligence services, President Jacques Chirac of France concluded that there were no weapons of mass destruction in Iraq.[15] However, John William the author of the first draft of The Iraq Dossier thought his role was to present the best case possible for war. There is no evidence that Blair asked for a contrary view of the data—the case against war. The Israeli government learnt this lesson in October 1973. Syria and Egypt launched a surprise attack on Israel—later known as the Yom Kippur War. There was clear, abundant information that this was imminent. But, due to prejudgments in the minds of leading intelligence officers, military and political leaders were not alerted. As a result, the government set up a devil's advocate group, whose role was to create contrary arguments to the prevailing assessment. The group still operates and has the right to report above the head of military intelligence.[16]

Blair could also have formed a decision group, as Kennedy did, to recommend a strategy. Since the legal case for war depended crucially on the existence of weapons of mass destruction, and Blair's red flags might cause him to misinterpret the intelligence data, a separate group could have provided the safeguard he needed. Most importantly, it would have allowed him to play a more detached governance role rather than that of war champion.

Which Projects to Cut?

The need for safeguards appears obvious when dealing with decisions that could lead to war. But they are also necessary in other settings.

One of the companies we worked with is an American electric utility. Let's call it Southwest UtiliCo. It faced a major change in the way it was regulated. Historically, expenditures were submitted for approval to the state regulatory authorities (the Public Utilities Commission, or PUC). Once they were approved, the utility was allowed to set prices that covered costs and provided a return on its investment. It seemed sensible: allowing the utility to earn a fair return while delivering a reasonably priced product.

The problem was that this arrangement wasn't working. The state had among the highest prices for electricity in the United States. Partly as a result, the PUC and parts of the state legislature had developed a very hostile attitude toward utilities—including Southwest. The utility could see that it had to find ways to bring prices down; otherwise, it could face punitive changes in regulation.

Corporate executives debated the issue and decided they needed to reduce the capital budget from $1 billion to $700 million: A draconian move that would allow them to hold prices steady. This required trimming back tens, if not hundreds, of different programs and canceling others. The executives scratched their heads. Which areas could and should be cut back? Which maintained? How should priorities be set? This was a new problem and the executive team did not know how to deal with it.

The traditional decision process involved submission of capital requests from the divisions (such as power generation and power distribution) and functions (such as IT and HR). Corporate leaders reviewed these for reasonableness. So far, so good. But, because corporate leaders did not understand the details of the business, they typically approved the expenditures or applied crude rules of thumb such as "keep growth in expenditures to 5 percent versus last year." Clearly, this approach was ill-suited to delivering a 30 percent cut.

There was another wrinkle. While corporate leaders had the ultimate power to authorize expenditures, the managers who proposed what to do were the heads of the businesses and functions. Unfortunately there were a number of red flag conditions likely to affect the judgment of these managers:

- **Misleading experiences.** Decisions about capital expenditure were affected by bad experiences from past failures of the power network—such as the forced shutdown of a power generation plant or the failure of some part of the power distribution grid. These failures typically led to highly negative reactions from customers, regulators, or the unions. The cumulative effect encouraged managers to overinvest in the utility infrastructure, so long as it could be justified to regulators. These experiences were potentially misleading because in the new regulatory environment, it was important to make more balanced trade-offs between cost and reliability.

- **Misleading prejudgments.** Most managers had been with the utility for a long time, during which they had developed a set of demanding engineering standards. Conformance to these standards was the main way in which investments were decided upon. Unfortunately, in an environment where prices would be capped, the engineering standards were potentially inappropriate.

- **Inappropriate self-interest.** The managers' worst nightmare was some sort of dramatic failure in their part of the company. Consequently, they were motivated to invest heavily in the network to try to reduce the risk of failure. Since the resulting increase in prices was not linked explicitly to individual investment decisions, there was little constraint on this behavior.

- **Inappropriate attachments.** Some managers treated their parts of the business as fiefdoms. Their focus was on keeping their management teams and workforces busy; one way of achieving this was to ensure a constant level of capital expenditure.

Overall, these red flags appeared to be distorting the decision process. Divisional and functional managers were proposing high levels of investment and corporate leaders did not know enough to challenge them. Initially, corporate leaders tried to find a way to analyze and prioritize the capital expenditure requests. But after trying to apply standard analytical approaches to the problem, they realized that this was an almost impossible task. Tools, such as payback or net present value analysis, were poor at ranking the merits of investments ranging from new power stations, to increased reliability in the power grid, to a new payroll system.

An alternative approach of simply increasing the time that corporate leaders spent discussing the investment proposals with the divisions and functions was also unlikely to work, because corporate leaders did not have the expertise required to provide an effective challenge. It would simply degenerate into a bureaucratic exercise.

Eventually, a new process was designed. At the heart of it was a new group which provided what we termed earlier, "Debate and Challenge." Each divisional and functional manager was required to join a capital prioritization committee. Each had to present their priorities to a panel of their peers, many of whom were customers for the services. For example, power generation investments provided power to maintain voltage levels on the distribution system. The high-voltage transmission grid business unit provided a service for both the power generation and the power distribution businesses. The IT department provided services to all the other departments, as did human resources. At the end of the presentations, the team went through a series of structured workshops to rank the value of investments proposed by their peers. Debate rapidly focused on a limited number of large projects, such as a new IT accounting system and an upgrade to a large coal-fired power station. Finally, the target was reached.

The proposed budget was then submitted to corporate leaders. The projects that had proved most marginal were debated further and some adjustments were made.

Some monitoring safeguards were added. For some projects, investment was split into phases. A post audit was made after the first phase of investment had been completed. Further expenditure was approved or cancelled depending on the results of the audit.

The consensus of the divisional and functional managers was that al-though it was a challenge to reach the $700 million target, it had been done successfully—eliminating expenditure that either was of limited benefit or could be delayed without detrimental side effects. The main role of the company's headquarters had been to present a credible logic for the $700 million target. From then on, the managers involved in spending the money took primary responsibility for cutting their collective budgets by 30 percent.

Alternatives to Safeguards

Safeguards, in the form of additions to the decision process, are not the only way to reduce the risk of a flawed decision—but in our view they are the most likely to be effective. One alternative is for decision makers to analyze their own biases and compensate for them. However, as the first eight chapters of this book illustrate, biases are often too deep rooted in emotions and in the unconscious to be objectively analyzed, especially by the individual concerned. Fighting millions of years of evolution is, to say the least, a challenge. To rely on self-analysis of red flags seems to us a worthy but insufficient solution. Although this appears self-evident to us, it appears that others do not share this view. A great deal of energy has gone into trying to find ways to reduce the bias exhibited by decision makers but, as a recent paper coauthored by Max Bazerman, a distinguished academic in this field, suggests, " . . . it is important to note how difficult finding solutions has proved to be."[17] He and his coauthors go on to suggest that ". . . our field primarily offers description about the biases that afflict decision makers without insights into how errors can be eliminated or at least reduced."[18] However, the types of solution they suggest are primarily aimed at making decision makers less susceptible to bias. We would humbly suggest that "the field" may be looking in the wrong place. It may prove more fruitful to research which process safeguards are most helpful in improving the quality of decisions, rather than ways to reduce the personal biases of decision makers.

Another alternative to safeguards is to try to change the context within which decisions are made. For example, changing the incentives and rewards for the decision maker can powerfully affect the way they evaluate options. The trouble is that changing the broad context for a specific decision can rarely be done in time and is rarely practical. For this reason, the four categories of safeguard seem to us the only practical solution that is generally available in the time frame of a particular decision. Safeguards do not need a long time to prepare, design, and implement. While bigger changes in the general organizational context are a powerful way to improve the quality of decisions, they are often not practical once a decision is clearly needed. We wish organizations were more malleable, but they are not.

Further information on safeguards is contained in appendix II and on our Web site, www.thinkagain-book.com.

Just Enough Process

Safeguards are all well and good, but they also have their downside. In particular, they can slow down the decision-making process. For example, Kennedy would have dearly loved to have known more about Soviet intentions, but there was no time for the intelligence services to gather information and conduct an appraisal. Another safeguard might have been to set up an additional review body to act as a governance mechanism over his own thinking. But it would have caused further delay, created bureaucracy, and potentially prejudiced the tight security around ExComm. Tony Blair, no doubt, felt that additional decision safeguards would have delayed the important work he was doing and reduced his flexibility.

The main challenge in identifying safeguards is to have *just enough* in place without jeopardizing efficient decision-making. It is necessary to use safeguards that are powerful and focused on counterbalancing the red flag conditions. But it is also necessary to avoid ones that have toxic side effects, such as delaying the decision or bogging it down in bureaucracy. Anyone with experience of large, bureaucratic organizations will be aware of the stifling nature of many decision processes. "More process" is not always "good process." Elaborate processes can quench motivation and kill initiative. Collecting all possible data can be costly, or delay decisions making them irrelevant. Kennedy could not postpone his decision about the missiles in Cuba, so he had to choose safeguards that were appropriate to the decision he faced.

Or consider the CEO of an international oil company who was exploring the effectiveness of his decision-making process. One recommendation was to increase the cohesiveness of the decision-making group by coaching team members on their contributions to debates. However, the CEO rejected this idea, favoring a more direct approach of acting as a strong chairman. He felt that the coaching approach was too "soft"—he wanted to develop a stronger culture. He wanted his subordinates to stand on their own feet without the benefit and (in his mind at least) the distraction of coaching.

Toxic effects can also dilute the power of a safeguard. An example is groupthink. The more a group bonds together, the more risk there is of the group becoming fixed on one way of thinking. Such groups may reduce the chance of good debate and challenge—precisely the opposite effect that is intended by using a group to make the decision.

Another type of toxic side effect is a lack of fit with the style of the decision maker or the decision-making group. For example, some senior decision makers prefer to debate major decisions behind closed doors with a handful of people—primarily in one-on-one discussions. Trying to introduce a more open process may be counterproductive or simply unacceptable. "We don't do things that way here" is a common rebuff to ideas for new safeguards.

Many decision makers are sensitive to toxic side effects and have an instinctive feel for what will and won't work. But using intuition creates a risk that a strong safeguard is rejected without consideration of the true impact of the side effects—or of ways in which these might be attenuated. For this reason, toxic side effects—whether real or perceived—are best dealt with by being explicit about them. It is best to lay out the costs and benefits of using a particular safeguard. If this trade-off is not explicitly recognized, safeguards may be dismissed for vague reasons—such as "I don't think that will work in our organization."

To reduce the risk of a flawed decision, we need to select safeguards that are powerful enough to counteract the distortions that may exist. Kennedy was concerned about the prejudgments that he and others might have about how to respond to the Cuban Missile Crisis. He needed to design a process with sufficient debate so that those prejudgments were vigorously challenged and debated. But he also needed to design a process that would not have excessive toxic side effects—such as taking too long to reach a decision.

This illustrates the fundamental challenge in selecting safeguards: *just enough* process is required. Enough—but only just enough. The right safeguards are those that powerfully address the specific red flag conditions of a particular decision, with manageable side effects. The worst decision processes may not always be those with too few safeguards but those that have too many.

How, then, do you select "just enough" safeguards? How do you judge how many you need and which ones are the best to use? How do you decide which are too burdensome? This is the topic of our next chapter.

TEN

Selecting Safeguards

I N THE PREVIOUS CHAPTER, we argued that the best way to reduce the risk of a flawed decision is to identify "just enough" safeguards. This is illustrated in figure 10-1.

Safeguards can help us avoid the effects of distorted thinking. Because of red flag conditions, we can place too much (or too little) weight on some aspects of the decision. Because we find it difficult to correct these distortions in our own minds, we need help. Safeguards act as counterbalances, reducing the risk of a bad decision. As we saw in chapter 9, these can take a number of forms—so a safeguard may expand the experience or information available to the decision maker; it may ensure that the logic of the decision is challenged and debated; it may have the power to reject proposals, as in the case of a governance safeguard; or, as a last resort, the safeguard may make it easier to change the decision if the early outcomes are unfavorable. Whatever form safeguards take, all have the same purpose: to reduce the risk of a flawed decision.

Of course, it is tempting to put safeguards in place regardless. Why not be as careful as possible? In practice, too much caution can be detrimental. The reason, as we explained earlier, is that too many safeguards—or the wrong sorts of safeguards—can have a toxic effect on decision making. You can overburden your decisions with too much

FIGURE 10-1

Safeguards can defend against the risk of error

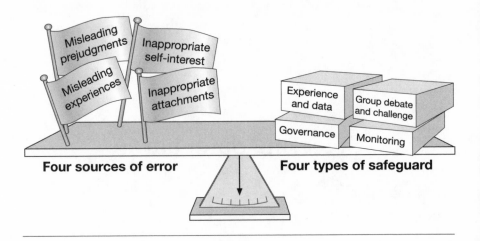

Four sources of error   Four types of safeguard

analysis, too many challenges, or too much governance. It is easy to fall into the trap of "pulling the tree up to see if the roots are growing." The art of choosing good safeguards is the art of just enough to counterbalance the red flags, but not too much to overburden the decision process.

So the next question is, how much is enough? How do you identify the right safeguards and then ensure that you don't kill the organization with too much bureaucracy? The rest of this chapter is an attempt to provide some practical advice. In doing so, we are only too well aware that different people have different needs. Some readers will have a great deal of experience in making decisions, while others are just starting out. In what follows, we try to cater to both groups—and those in between as well.

The first point to make is that the need for safeguards depends on the red flags. For example, if a decision maker has had a misleading experience that might bias his or her decision, it may be enough to provide that individual with some new data. But if the decision maker has several very important personal interests at stake in the decision, only a strong governance process can counterbalance the risks of bias. So the first step in picking safeguards is to understand the red flag conditions.

The second step is to pick safeguards that will work well with the people concerned. Some safeguards will be ineffective or have more negatives than positives. For example, a very aggressive challenge process can be powerful, and some companies develop a culture in which strong challenge is a natural part of a decision process. However, in a different organization with different individuals, a strong challenge process might lead to excessive conflict or demotivate the decision makers.

Overall, the process of selecting safeguards involves being clear about the red flag conditions, thinking about the context, and then selecting some safeguards that will work in this situation with these people.

Some leaders need no more guidance than this: as experienced decision makers, they can intuitively select safeguards. Others, however, find it helpful to use a more structured approach. This may be because the situation is particularly complex or because they have limited experience in designing decision processes. In the examples below, we consider both intuitive and more structured approaches to selecting safeguards.

Using Intuition to Select Safeguards

In many situations, an experienced decision maker can intuitively work out what safeguards are needed. For example, a large U.K. chemical company (let's call it InvestCo) was considering a major investment in Russia. The chairman was concerned that the CEO and the regional management team had become overcommitted to the project. In this case, the chairman had not done a formal red flags analysis, but if he had, he might have been concerned about prejudgments. For example, he was concerned that local managers had presumed that the market was attractive. He was also concerned about attachments. Local managers had close and difficult-to-unwind relationships with local partners. The chairman also recognized that his own thinking could be biased. He had previous experiences of losing money in Russia and had recently been briefed about deteriorating relationships between Russia and the United Kingdom.

Faced with these concerns, the chairman considered how to intervene. He did not want to unbalance the decision by imposing his own experiences on the decision process, but was concerned that the regional management team might be under the influence of red flag conditions. He decided to intervene in a couple of ways. First, he shared his concerns with the CEO. Next, the chairman suggested to the CEO that some additional due diligence might be needed on this decision. He proposed that the regional management team should spend some time in Russia working with the local partner before finalizing the proposal for the board. He also decided that if the regional managers were still enthusiastic about the project, he would arrange for them and the CEO to have the same briefing that he had received about government relations between the United Kingdom and Russia. Both of these interventions were forms of safeguard: they strengthened the decision process in ways that might rebalance the thinking of the regional managers if they were suffering from misleading experiences, misleading prejudgments, or inappropriate attachments. As it turns out, the caution evident in the chairman's reaction proved to be a sufficient safeguard in itself. The management team reconsidered and decided not to proceed with the project.

In this case, the chairman diagnosed the situation and came up with some safeguards intuitively. He didn't need an elaborate process of analysis. For managers sensitized to the risks of flawed thinking and to the need to tailor decision processes to offset the risks, the process of spotting red flags and choosing safeguards is not difficult. Of course, this requires a reservoir of knowledge and experiences often acquired over many years— and sometimes informed by previous costly mistakes. That is the nature of judgment—it is often hard earned. But this does not imply that only experienced senior managers can select safeguards for important decisions. Although it helps if you have years of experience to fall back on, even relatively inexperienced decision makers can evaluate and choose safeguards. But it may require them to take a more structured approach.

Adding Some Structure

Let's say that you are not quite as experienced as the chairman in the example above. So what can you do to minimize the risks of a bad decision? Drawing on the framework described earlier, you can structure your thinking by asking yourself the following two questions. First, are there any red flag conditions; and if so, how might they unbalance the decision? Second, what safeguards might counterbalance the effects of the most worrying red flags?

To illustrate the more structured approach, let's apply these questions (briefly) to the Boots example presented in chapter 6. (We examine the same example in more detail on our Web site, www.thinkagain-book.com, to illustrate how to apply the framework in a more analytical way.)

Steve Russell, chief executive of Boots from 2000 to 2004, faced the decision about how to strengthen the company's core drugstore business and how to grow the company. He chose to focus on the company's health and beauty positioning and to reinforce the positioning with additional businesses in health-care services such as dentistry, opticians, chiropody, and other well-being services. While the first half of the strategy was successful, the additional health-care businesses were not. Let's put ourselves in the position of the chairman of Boots, prior to the decision.

Are there any red flag conditions, and how might they unbalance the decision? As discussed in chapter 6, Russell had a potentially misleading and strong prejudgment that Boots needed to grow and that health-care services were an attractive opportunity.

Russell also had a number of potentially misleading experiences. For example, Boots had enjoyed a competitive advantage in retail pharmacy due to its scale. However, scale did not necessarily apply in some of the health-care services that he wanted to enter, such as dentistry.

Russell also had some inappropriate self-interest in the decision. A growth option, such as expanding into a range of health-care services, was more personally attractive to him than options such as sticking to the core business or selling the company. As he explained, "Frankly, if the board had wanted to follow a cash strategy, they would have had to do it without me."[1]

Russell may also have had some inappropriate attachments to the Boots retail management team, the Boots brand and organization. In his words, "My concern was that the company was on the verge of becoming bereft of hope or ambition."

Overall, then, Russell was likely to favor options involving growth into health-care services—particularly those that leveraged the Boots brand and the retail business. Moreover, Russell was likely to be against lower-growth options, such as reinvesting in the core business. This bias could have been quite strong. In Russell's own words, "I had been formulating this ambition for Boots since I was merchandising director of Boots the Chemist in the late 1980s. So, when I became CEO, I was determined to make it happen."

What safeguards might counterbalance the effects of the most worrying red flags? Putting yourself in the position of the chairman of Boots, you can see that Russell might be right—but because the circumstances may have changed since Russell first formed his view, there is a red flag. Moreover, Russell has no experience in health-care services, so he could easily misjudge the opportunity. So what can you do?

Your task is to identify the best safeguards to counterbalance the biases that Russell may have. But how do you select the best combination of safeguards? As we show in appendix II, there are tens, if not hundreds, of potential safeguards to choose from. Let's consider some safeguards that might be helpful:

- **Experience, data, and analysis.** Exposing Russell to new experiences or data might cause him to challenge his own prejudgments. This could fix the problem at the source. As chairman, you might encourage Russell to get some personal experience in these health-care businesses. You might also recommend that he commission a consultant to report on the market size, profitability, competitors, and core competences needed in each area of the market. However, given the strength of Russell's views, it appears unlikely that this alone will be powerful enough to eliminate the bias toward the health-care services strategy.

- **Debate and challenge.** If you cannot rely on new experience, data, and analysis to do the job, you might recommend to Russell that he strengthen his decision team with someone who has worked in health-care services. To do so successfully, it will be necessary to find someone with the relevant expertise and sufficient strength of character to challenge Russell.

  An alternative would be to suggest that, given Russell's pre-judgment, he should set up a separate team to examine the case against entering these markets. If this team were to report directly to a governance body consisting of Russell and other board members, it might be independent enough to deliver an objective analysis of the options.

  However, a potential problem with this approach is that Russell has already declared that the health-care services strategy is the option that he would like to pursue. Separating him from the analysis and development of this strategy, in order to challenge it, is something that is demotivating and, in practice, may be impossible to achieve.

- **Governance.** If you feel that neither the data nor the decision team and process are powerful enough on their own to counter-balance Russell's prejudgments, you could consider strengthening the governance process. You might set up a special subcommittee of the board to review the proposal in detail—supported perhaps by an independent consultant working directly for the subcommittee.

- **Monitoring.** Finally, since there is a danger that all these safe-guards are still insufficient, it will probably be sensible to make sure that the monitoring process is beefed up. If the wrong decision is made, it will be important to spot the error early and change course. For example, you could personally spend extra time monitoring early progress, meeting the people leading new health-care initiatives, and checking with industry observers. You could ensure that clear milestones for performance are set, monitored, and acted on.

As it turns out, these steps were not taken (otherwise, the case would not have appeared in this book). One reason was that the Boots chairman had been the previous CEO and was involved in promoting Russell. He may have felt less willing to challenge Russell than if he had been a truly independent chairman. Moreover, some of the early problems that were encountered were not fully reported to Russell, let alone the board. The individuals leading these initiatives knew that Russell was committed to them, and did not want to disillusion him by sharing the bad news.

The problems Boots faced in selecting and implementing appropriate safeguards illustrate some very real challenges. Even if we suspect that the decision maker may be inappropriately biased, effective safeguards may be hard to put in place. And the full extent and importance of the red flag conditions may not be clear. What we are proposing is not a panacea, but a way of improving your odds. Providing a method for spotting red flag conditions and choosing safeguards will not eliminate flawed decisions, but it can reduce their risk. As Russell himself said when he read through sections of our draft manuscript, he wished he had had it at the time!

Picking Safeguards in More Complex Situations

Sometimes the task of identifying appropriate safeguards can appear daunting—even for an experienced chairman. First, the decision itself may be unclear, making it hard to think about red flags. Second, the number of people involved in the decision can be large, making it hard to assess all the potential red flags or creating a long list of red flags associated with the different people involved. For example, consider the following case.

A team had been appointed to evaluate whether to move the corporate headquarters of a large, family-controlled European industrial company from southern Germany to a new location. There were a number of options, including staying in southern Germany, moving to another location in Europe, or even moving to Asia, to take advantage of its lower cost base and because this was a rapidly developing market for the company.

The potential savings were significant due to the large number of current employees and their high cost. Also, the current location was some distance from a major airport, so a new location could reduce traveling time and costs significantly. On the other hand, many of the senior employees had settled in Germany and might leave the company or be less motivated if the headquarters were moved to another country. It was unclear whether the service levels and effectiveness of various functions, such as HR, would be affected if they were separated from the top management team.

Several individuals and groups were involved in the decision, including the chief executive, the management committee, the chairman of the board, and major family shareholders who also sat on the board. The chief executive, based in Germany, headed the management committee, which was also the steering group for the decision. One member of the committee, the former head of a region who was close to retiring, had been appointed as project leader.

The chief executive had been in the post for one year, having spent many years with the company. Although he was German by birth, his job previous to his appointment was in the United States, and he had held other overseas posts. During the year, he had made a series of organizational changes, winnowing out some senior executives and appointing several people who had worked with him during his prior postings to the management committee. The chief executive had frequently discussed the importance of having a happy and effective team, and had stated that the effectiveness of the team must be an important criterion in the decision. He had privately expressed some concern that moving the headquarters, an idea originally suggested by the chairman, might have several unintended and unfortunate consequences. He was determined that these should be assessed carefully before proceeding.

The business was controlled by a family-owned holding company based in London. The influence of the holding company had traditionally been rather limited, but the family had decided that it needed to exert more pressure on business performance. They had recently hired a new chairman to help them do this. He had come from a major U.K. company and had a strong track record in improving performance—albeit as a senior executive in individual business units rather than in a holding company position. Prior to his position in the U.K. company, the chairman had captained a nuclear submarine; he was known for his clear but sometimes autocratic management style. He visited Germany frequently and had an apartment there, but his family still lived in London.

The chairman had been asked by some of the family members on the board to be active in making the headquarters decision. He had expressed the view that headquarters costs were high, although he also said that he wanted the evaluation process to be objective and thorough. He had attended a couple of early meetings about the project, and, in the words of one of the management committee members, "his body language was not very friendly."

The project leader had worked in Germany for many years, and had children at school there and a chalet in the mountains he and his family visited on the weekend. He claimed to speak for other management committee members when he expressed a desire to stay in situ. As he put it, "It is alright for me—I will probably retire. But my colleagues might have to face some tough personal decisions if we move." Other management committee members maintained that they were open to all options.

———————

Given this situation, how easy is it to identify the red flags and decide how to tailor the decision process? First, who is the decision maker? The project leader is responsible for coming up with a recommendation, but the chief executive is clearly going to be very influential in the decision— as is the chairman. In addition, some of the family members might decide to become involved. Whose red flags should you be considering?

A second uncertainty is about the framing of the decision. The project leader has been asked to decide, "Where should headquarters be located?" But a second decision that will need to be made is, "How many people should this new headquarters contain?" Perhaps both these ways of framing the decision are too narrow. Maybe a better framing would be, "What should the role of HQ be?" Only when that has been answered can questions about size and location be properly addressed.

The red flags will be very different depending on the framing, so which framing should you consider?

Clearly, for someone who does not have a wealth of experience in high-level decision making, the complexity of the situation makes it difficult to identify appropriate safeguards. Where should we start? Are there any tips worth knowing?

The rest of this chapter offers some practical guidance. Our aim is to show that it is possible to apply the red flags and safeguards thinking even to complex decisions. What we present below is not rocket science. In fact, it is the opposite. It is simple common sense. The thought process you need is not clever, or counterintuitive. As the four recommendations below illustrate, it is simple, direct, and something you can do right away.

1. Keep It Simple—Then Iterate

Our general advice is, keep it simple at first—then iterate on your first answer. If you start with what seems to be a reasonable approach you can build on it later—revising your analysis to factor in some of the real complexities of the situation. The point is that you have to start from somewhere and then work from there.

Take the example of the headquarters decision described above. One of the complexities was that there were several people with an influence on the decision, including the project leader, the chief executive, the chairman of the board, and family members. Do you have to identify the red flags of all these people? No—pick one to start with! For example, the chief executive seems likely to be an important influence on the decision, so let us begin by analyzing his red flags. We can always analyze the red flags of others later.

There were similar complexities about what the real decision was. Was it, "Where should headquarters be located?" "How many people should this new headquarters contain?" or "What should the role of HQ be?" Again, pick one. The simplest one to start with is the current framing: "Where should headquarters be located?" Later on, you can go back to consider the implications of the alternative ways of framing the decision.

Now that you have chosen a decision maker and a decision, it is a much more manageable task to think through the red flags and some possible safeguards. If we consider the red flag conditions of the chief executive, facing the decision of "Where to locate headquarters," one is his potential attachment to the existing management team. This could cause him to favor the option of remaining in Germany.

On the "keep it simple" principle, let's start with just this one red flag. You might consider safeguards, such as appointing someone to the steering committee who will champion the option of moving away from Germany.

You can now iterate back to identify other red flags and consider whether this safeguard would be appropriate for them. For example, the chief executive has also expressed privately some concern about moving the headquarters. This may be based on an informed and objective evaluation of the options. However, if he has reached this view without a proper consideration of all the other options, it may also be a misleading prejudgment. Fortunately, the safeguard we have already considered would also counterbalance this second red flag.

Having come up with an initial view of how to safeguard the decision against possible distortions in the mind of the CEO, you can now iterate back to consider some of the other decision makers. For example, the chairman is also likely to have a significant influence on the decision. His red flags include a potential prejudgment that the headquarters is too big and should be moved out of Germany. Fortunately this red flag is a counterbalance to those of the chief executive. Including the chairman and the chief executive on the steering committee might therefore guard against the red flag conditions of both individuals. But anticipating a clash of opinions (and egos), you may consider it prudent to add some facilitation to the process—to ensure that the debate is constructive and effective and does not become personal.

The point we are making is that by starting with one decision maker and one framing, you can begin analyzing a complex decision. You can select some safeguards and then refine your choice by considering further decision makers and framings. For example, in addition to the chairman, you could now also consider the red flag conditions pertaining to the project leader and to family members. Given these additional red flags, do the safeguards you are coming up with appear adequate? If not, you will need to consider others.

At this point you have only considered one framing for the decision: "Where to locate headquarters." Perhaps the chief executive and project leader have a misleading prejudgment that this is the best way to frame the decision. Do we need additional safeguards against this red flag? In this case, probably not. If the chairman is added to the steering committee, it is likely that the decision process will consider alternative ways of framing the decision, such as "Is the headquarters too large?" If you have concerns, however, you might suggest an additional safeguard, such as making sure that the project leader organizes a discussion of alternative frames with the steering committee—to ensure that a broad range of alternative framings get aired and debated.

Note that you don't need to know which framing is the right one. Perhaps it is right to stick with the original framing—or perhaps it is better to expand the frame. All you need to identify is that it would be appropriate for the decision process to consider a range of frames, and make sure that prejudged opinions are balanced with other views.

So by starting with one decision maker and one framing, you can come up with ideas for safeguards, around which you can iterate your thinking. You don't need to think about all the decision makers or all the alternative framings before coming up with some suggested safeguards. You don't need to know who the most important decision maker is or which is the best frame. Start somewhere sensible and iterate.

Another complexity you may face is that you don't know enough about the decision makers to make as detailed a diagnosis of red flags as you would like. Following the "keep it simple" principle, do an initial analysis and then go and discuss it with others. Indeed, even if you feel that you are quite well informed, the implications of our "one plan at a time" decision process are that you might, for example, think of the chief executive as the main decision maker and forget about the potential influence of the chairman. Discussing your diagnosis of red flags and proposed changes to the decision process with others is a great way to challenge and improve your selection of safeguards.

So our general advice is, start simply and iterate to deal with the apparent complexities of the situation.

2. Start with the Most Worrying Red Flag

You may find that you have a long list of red flags to consider. When we ask people to identify red flags for their decisions, they sometimes come up with two or three for each of the four categories of red flag conditions. Analyzing the safeguards required for each of these seems a daunting task. Where to start?

Following the overall advice of "keep it simple," start with what you feel will be the most worrying red flag.

How do you sense that a red flag condition is worrying? Intuition may suffice—but it may be helpful to describe what is going on inside our brains when we do this. We construct a movie in our mind of how the red flag condition might influence the decision maker to favor certain options over others. We assess whether the difference between the options chosen and the options not chosen is a significant one. We don't have to decide which is the "right" option—only that the red flag might result in a significant bias in the option chosen and hence a significant difference in the outcome.

For example, in the headquarters case, the chief executive has several red flags. We have already mentioned his potential attachment to the existing management team and his potential prejudgment that a headquarters move would be a bad idea. But these are not his only red flags. He has a potential self-interest in not having to move his family and home from Germany. He might also have some self-interest in keeping the headquarters away from the chairman and the family members— so that he can retain tight control of his management team.

The first of these, the attachment to his team, is worrying. It might influence the chief executive to choose to remain in Germany rather than move. The effect of this would be significant, as the potential cost savings from moving is tens of millions of euros per annum. Overall, we assess this to be a worrying red flag and therefore a reasonable one to start with. (The assessment may be arrived at intuitively or analytically.)

Once you have chosen a red flag, think through which safeguards might be most appropriate for that red flag. Then go back and pick another worrying red flag, and ask whether the safeguards that you have already chosen will be adequate to protect against that as well.

Now that you have dealt with what to do when there are many red flags, the next challenge is how to choose between the many possible safeguards. (Here we have referred primarily to only one safeguard: including the chairman on the steering committee. But in appendix II, we provide checklists of the many safeguards available.) How do you select which will be most appropriate for a given decision maker and red flag condition?

3. If in Doubt, Consider Safeguards in Order

To choose between a large number of alternative safeguards, follow the sequence hinted at in the previous chapter and summarized in figure 10-2. First, think about *new experiences and data*. Can these give the decision maker a broader set of patterns and emotional tags to draw on? If that does not seem sufficient, consider how *debate and challenge* might help the decision maker to rebalance his or her thinking. If real debate and challenge is hard to imagine, because, for example, the decision maker is a dominant individual, the next area in which to look for safeguards is the *governance process*. Can governance be strengthened so that any flawed proposals are rejected? Finally, if you are still concerned that the decision may be flawed, think about ways to strengthen the *monitoring process* so that the results of a flawed decision are spotted and addressed as early and effectively as possible.

Consider the headquarters case again. You have already identified some red flag conditions that might affect the judgment of the chief executive. These include potentially inappropriate attachments to his

FIGURE 10-2

Choosing safeguards

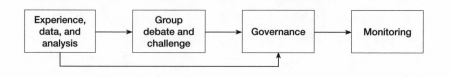

management team and a misleading prejudgment against a move of headquarters. Might data and analysis help counterbalance these issues in the chief executive's mind? Probably not. Both of these red flags may have strong emotional tags that are unlikely to be counterbalanced just by more information. However, debate and challenge through the decision group might be an effective safeguard, especially if it were achieved by including the chairman on the steering committee and adding a facilitator to the process.

If you still have concerns, you could add a further layer of governance. You could set up a special subcommittee of the main board of the holding company to review the output of the steering committee. Maybe you could ask an independent consultant to do an analysis of different options—to help the board members review the decision objectively.

Finally, if you were concerned that even extra governance might not be enough to prevent a flawed decision, then you could consider how a monitoring process might help. In this case, you would probably conclude that tighter monitoring would be a poor safeguard. Once a change in location has been decided on, it is unlikely that there will be a chance to correct the decision quickly should it prove flawed. This would cause you to return to the other safeguards and think harder about how to make them effective.

At the end of this review of alternatives, you may have identified several potentially interesting safeguards. Does this mean that you should use all these safeguards? Intuitively, you sense that this might be overkill. But how do you tell when you have too many safeguards? How many are enough? How many are too many, or too few? This brings us to our fourth and final recommendation.

4. Weigh the Benefits of Each Safeguard Against Its Toxic Side Effects

You have identified a number of possible safeguards—but how do you choose between them? You have to assess first whether they have sufficient power to counterbalance the potential effects of the red flags. But you also have to assess whether they have any negative effects—what we call toxic side effects. An analogy is when a doctor prescribes medicine. There may be several drugs to choose from. The doctor will consider the effects of the disease (the biases that might result from the red flag conditions), the degree to which the drugs target the particular disease (whether the safeguards will target these specific biases), the potency of the drugs (the strength of the various safeguards), and their potential toxic side effects (whether the safeguard has any negative impacts that might outweigh its benefits).

In the case of the headquarters decision, there are several potential safeguards. These include:

- Adding the chairman, a family member, some operating managers, an independent expert, or a facilitator to the steering committee

- Creating a special subcommittee of the board of the holding company to provide additional governance

- Hiring an independent consultant to evaluate the different locations

Reviewing these, you can consider which are the most attractive—in other words, which most powerfully target the red flag conditions and have limited side effects. For example, inserting the chairman into the decision process is a powerful safeguard—the chairman has significant experience and authority. He is willing to challenge the chief executive if needed. However, his interventions are not particularly targeted at the red flag conditions—for example, they will not directly address the chief executive's attachment to his management team. Also, there may be some toxic side effects—for example, any personal rivalry between the two individuals might be heightened. Perhaps the escalation of the argument would create an unpleasant and damaging standoff. A facilitator may help, or you may want to consider arranging some meetings between the two of them outside the steering committee. Overall, this safeguard is analogous to a powerful drug whose side effects you may need to manage.

Thinking about this might trigger you to consider an alternative safeguard, with less toxic side effects. For example, it might be helpful to find out how much the chief executive's thinking is affected by attachments. For example, the project leader could talk to the chief executive about the factors influencing his thinking. If his attachments to the management team seem to have little influence, it may not be necessary to involve the chairman in the process. Maybe the project team's work will provide sufficient counterbalance on its own, or maybe an explicit discussion of the likely impact on the management team will bring the issue to the table, where it can be debated more objectively.

We have now taken you through the process of identifying appropriate safeguards. You may face complexities and challenges along the way—but there are ways to deal with these. We have illustrated this using an example that has some of the complexity and subtlety of real life—with different ways to frame the decision, several individuals who might have an influence on the decision, and multiple red flags.

Our intention in this chapter has been to provide you with a range of approaches for identifying red flags and selecting safeguards—and some ideas about how to use this thinking in your daily lives. Whether you use your own intuition or some of our recommendations, we hope that you now have the capability to think through whether your decision needs additional safeguards, and what those might be. For further ideas, see our Web site, www.thinkagain-book.com. Our own experiences suggest this will improve your chances of coming up with the right answer when facing important decisions.

Becoming an effective decision maker is not just about being an expert and having good judgment—it is also about taking steps to guard against the inevitable distortions and biases that can lead to a flawed decision. You can never eliminate all flawed decisions—but you can reduce the risk.

ELEVEN

Leaders Make Good Decisions

DECISIONS ARE THE LIFEBLOOD of action, in organizations and for individuals. Without them, little gets done. Yet decisions can be complex, and we are never going to get everything right. Even the best-thought-out plans by the most rational and unemotional decision makers don't always turn out perfectly. This book cannot ensure that you will win every time—no book can. But what if someone were to come to you and say:

- "It *is* possible to get better at decision making, and keep getting better."

- "There are specific and identifiable places to look, ahead of time, before things turn out badly."

- "There are specific and identifiable actions you can take, ahead of time, to significantly reduce your risk of making bad decisions."

That is what this book is all about. Relying on extensive research by others on neuroscience and on decision making, and our own database on strategic decisions, we can now offer a realistic road map toward more powerful, lower-risk decisions.

Consider the possibilities. What if Matthew Broderick at the Department of Homeland Security had understood that New Orleans was not Florida, and a hurricane was not the military battlefield? That when he underestimated the catastrophic damage of Katrina, he was really relying on an experience base that was dangerously misleading? Broderick, like An Wang, allowed himself to believe he was right when he was really wrong. He did not think again, and made a decision that contributed to the disaster that was Katrina.

Many of us can look back at important decisions in which we played a key role, and regardless of how it turned out, can probably recall times when our thoughts and actions did not perfectly align with the reality of the situation. Perhaps it was when we blindly drew upon past experience without fully considering the relevance of that experience to the decision we were confronting. Perhaps it was when we locked onto a solution and refused to consider alternative views because of a powerful prejudgment or attachment.

Or consider the position of the chairman of Boots at the time when Steve Russell made the flawed decision to enter health-care services. What if he had understood better that prejudgments were potentially distorting Russell's decision making? What if he had thought again about the decision process and added some safeguards, such as a subcommittee of the board or a more rigorous monitoring process?

Many of us can look back at important decisions that seemed, in hindsight at least, to be like a slow-motion film of a runaway train. We sensed that people's biases were influencing the outcome. We felt uncomfortable. But we didn't do enough to analyze the potential problems and recommend safeguards.

On other occasions, we were driving the train. In looking back, we may wonder, why did this happen? Why did I allow myself to become so biased or fixated on a solution? Why did I think I was right, when the truth is, I was probably wrong? Why did I not think more creatively about how to strengthen the decision process? Why did I not think again?

If we take to heart the lessons from this book, there are only two conclusions we can draw:

1. I didn't realize it was happening while it was happening.

2. I will do whatever it takes to make sure it doesn't happen again.

I Didn't Realize It Was Happening

We have discussed at length the fascinating research in neuroscience on the power of our subconscious and its ability to drive not only our thinking but also our behavior. This is all true, but does the power of our subconscious give us a "get out of jail free" card, essentially absolving us of responsibility? Absolutely not! Think about how many times decisions are made in your organization, or your team, or even your family, without open discussion of what people are really thinking? So why are we surprised that bad decisions are made?

Now, we cannot make sure that people always speak up, and even if they do, we cannot make sure that those with power will pay any attention. So what can we do? We can help people realize what is happening. Do you live in an organization where it is common for managers to talk about red flag conditions and the need to safeguard the decision process? For most, the answer is no. This means that we don't put ourselves in a position to realize that something bad might be happening. Hence we have little chance of stopping it from happening.

But now you are armed with an understanding of the brain, a list of four red flag conditions that can be spotted in advance of a decision, and some ideas for safeguards that might counterbalance the red flags. You now have no excuse. You now need to use this knowledge to spot decisions that might go wrong, and speak up.

I Will Do Whatever It Takes to Make Sure It Doesn't Happen Again

As we go around the world working with companies and giving speeches to various groups, it is remarkable how often audiences are nodding their heads in agreement with our points, and saying how An

Wang, or Paul Wolfowitz, or whoever, really blew it. It is always easier to see what others have done wrong, but nothing can change until we take personal responsibility for how decisions are made in our organizations or teams.

How do we spot the red flag traps that can distort our thinking? When someone makes it his or her priority to diagnose the red flags in any decision situation. How do we combat the red flags and strengthen our decision-making processes? When someone makes it his or her priority to build in safeguards, in advance of the decision (or at least early on in the process). The bottom line is that it is our responsibility to face up to the possibility that dangerous biases exist, and to act to safeguard the decision.

The red flags and safeguards process isn't a panacea. Perhaps you are concerned that you will not be able to identify all the red flag conditions. Perhaps you are concerned that powerful enough safeguards are not available. Perhaps, indeed, there is no way to effectively safeguard the decision.

While these concerns are all natural, there is another, more positive way of thinking. You probably can already sense some red flag conditions that exist. If not, you may be able to identify them by discussing the decision with those involved. Once you have spotted a red flag and shared your concerns with others, together you will almost certainly be able to think of a suitable safeguard. If not, our safeguard framework, appendix II, or Web site should help.

Important decisions are too important for you to sit back and hope they will go well. If you are involved, you have a responsibility to help make the best decision possible.

Leaders Make Good Decisions

At the heart of our analysis is the premise that leaders can make good decisions. But to do so, we need to broaden our understanding of what happens when we are confronted with the usual mix of unstructured and incomplete data, different perspectives, time pressures, and other sources of uncertainty. In many companies, there is a tendency to treat strategic decisions as primarily rational processes of analysis. An organization faces a particular context defined in terms of competitors, customers, suppliers, regulators, and other stakeholders, and seeks ways to best position itself to meet its core objectives. For example, when Motorola looked out at its changing business landscape in the mobile phone business in the 1990s, it would have seen Nokia and Ericsson shifting from analog to digital technologies, would have looked internally to see that it had some of the key capabilities for digital, and would have quickly moved to take advantage of these key capabilities to push into a strong position in digital mobile telephony. Certainly, any business school student or strategy analyst worth his salt would have seen this strategy as the "obvious" business move at the time. The only problem with this standard analysis, however, is that it ignores arguably the single most important part of the picture: the decision makers! Motorola managers that had bet on analog continued to look for data to support their existing strategy, citing "43 million analog customers can't be wrong" as evidence to continue on the wrong path.[1] Decisions don't just happen by themselves and don't take form in some random way. "Objective strategic analysis" is close to useless if the key decision makers are not part of that analysis.

That's why it is so important to bring the focus back to the key people—the leaders of organizations. Leaders have the responsibility to ensure that those involved in an important decision *are* part of the analysis. Leaders also have the responsibility to be open to the possibility that they too may lack objectivity.

But what an opportunity we have! Almost everyone spends a big part of their work life in organizations. Many people also dedicate significant time to volunteering and other activities that take place in an organizational setting. So all of us have been involved in decision making and have seen others make decisions that affect us in important ways. Imagine what might be possible if we took to heart what we know about people and decisions. If we actively pay attention to the red flag conditions that often lie beneath the surface. And if we actively focus on safeguards to counterbalance those red flags. There is a huge opportunity for improvement.

At the end of day, mistakes and disasters will occur. Understanding the lessons of this book cannot guarantee that we will never be part of such bad outcomes, or even that bad decisions will never occur on our watch. But the lessons of this book can reduce our vulnerability and help us avoid some of those bad decisions that may destroy our organizations, careers, or even lives. We all have the capacity to "think again"—the only question is whether we will do so.

Database of Cases

THIS APPENDIX lists the cases we have researched (see table AI-1), dividing them between cases where we had interviews with the people concerned and those where we relied entirely on publicly available data. In some cases, such as that of Hurricane Katrina and Blair's decision to go to war in Iraq, the publicly available information is very extensive.

Each case has then been scored against the four main causes of decision errors.

- "Major" means the factor was probably a major cause.

- "Some" means the factor probably had some influence.

- "Limited" means the factor probably had some, but very limited, influence.

- "?" means we do not have enough information to make a judgment.

- "-" means the factor probably had no influence.

Where significant other influences were at work, these are listed in the "Comments and other" column.

TABLE AI-1

Database of cases

Cases	Misleading experiences	Misleading prejudgment	Self-interest	Attach-ment	Comments and other
Based on interviews					
1. Boots—health-care services	Some	Major	Some	Limited	
2. Rentokil—major acquisitions	Major	Some	Some	Some	
3. Marconi—decision not to sell the company	Some	?	Major	Some	
4. Boots—taking stores international	Major	Major	Some	Some	
5. Boots—organization decision	—	?	—	Some	Bad advice from expert
6. Confidential—acquisition	?	Major	Some	Some	
7. NatWest—development of markets business	—	Major	Some	Some	
8. NatWest—development of life business	Major	Major	Some	Some	
9. ITV—development of On Digital	—	Major	Limited	Some	
10. Philips A—confidential	Major	Major	Some	—	Government influence
11. Philips B—confidential	Major	Some	Some	—	Greener pastures problem
12. Unilever—project to become more innovative	—	Major	Some	—	
13. Unilever—focus on 400 brands	Some	Major	—	—	Bad advice
14. Reuters—slow response to market changes	Major	Major	—	—	
15. TI Group—EIS acquisition	Some	Major	Major	—	
16. Food company—brand manager	Major	Limited	Major	—	
17. Consulting business centralization	Limited	—	Major	Major	
18. New CEO for Indian family company	Major	Some	Some	Some	
19. Charitable foundation—investment in new program	Major	Some	Limited	—	
20. Charitable foundation—appointment of museum director	—	Some	Major	Some	

(continued)

TABLE AI-1 *(continued)*

Database of cases

Cases	Misleading experiences	Misleading prejudgment	Self-interest	Attach-ment	Comments and other
Based on interviews (continued)					
21. Power company— entry into Europe	Some	Major	Major	—	
22. Boston Red Sox— racial integration	—	Major	Major	—	
23. Fruit of the Loom— move manufacturing offshore	Some	—	Some	Major	
24. General Magic— commercialize new PDA technology in early 1990s	Some	Major	Some	Major	
25. Iridium—build out satellite telecom	—	Major	Major	Major	
26. Johnson & Johnson (J&J) Stent—next-generation stent	—	Major	Major	—	
27. J&J—integrate Cordis	Major	Some	Major	Some	
28. Motorola—digital technology	Some	Major	Major	Some	
29. Oxford—IT conversion	Major	Some	Limited	Limited	
30. Rubbermaid—manage distribution change	Major	Some	Some	Major	
31. Saatchi & Saatchi— expansion	Major	Some	Major	Limited	
32. Schwinn—enter new mountain biking segment	Some	—	—	Major	
33. Snow Brand—product contamination	Limited	—	Major	Limited	
34. Toro—manufacture snowblowers without snow	Some	Major	—	—	
35. Webvan—aggressive growth strategy	Major	Some	Major	—	
36. GM—automation	Limited	Major	Some	—	
37. An Wang—PC decision	Major	Major	—	Major	
38. Samsung—entry into cars	Some	Some	—	Major	
39. Quaker—acquisition of Snapple	Major	Some	—	—	
40. Mattel—brand extension	Major	Major	—	—	
41. Blair's decision to go to war in Iraq	Major	Major	Some	Limited	

(continued)

TABLE AI-1 (*continued*)

Database of cases

Cases	Misleading experiences	Misleading prejudgment	Self-interest	Attachment	Comments and other
Based on interviews (continued)					
42. Consumer goods company—new distribution system	Major	—	—	—	
43. U.S. bank expansion of independent investment advisory business	—	Major	Major	Major	
44. European company moving location of HQ	—	Major	Some	Major	
45. Pharmaceuticals company continuation of investment in new drug	—	Some	Major	—	
46. U.S. utility reduction in capital investment	Some	Major	Major	Some	
47. IPP entering deregulation	Major	Major	Major	Some	
48. Disguised company— new strategy	Some	Major	Some	—	
49. Disguised company— acquisition	—	Some	Major	—	
Based on public data					
1. Battle of Midway	Major	Major	Limited	—	
2. Alfred Russel Wallace and spiritualism	Major	Major	Some	—	
3. Leverrier and Vulcan	Major	Major	Some	—	
4. President Hoover and the great crash	Major	Major	—	—	
5. Daimler—acquisition of Chrysler	?	Major	Some	Some	Bad strategic thinking
6. Kerkorian's offer for Chrysler	Major	Major	—	—	
7. Daimler decision to integrate with Mercedes	—	?	Some	—	
8. Cendant merger	Major	Major	Major	—	
9. DEC—organization decision	Major	Limited	—	—	
10. DEC—growth	—	Major	Some	—	
11. Disguised case— low cost strategy	Major	Major	Major	—	
12. Lafarge—gypsum technology	—	Major	Some	Major	
13. T. Eaton Co.—failed turnaround	—	—	Some	Some	

(continued)

TABLE AI-1 (*continued*)

Database of cases

Cases	Misleading experiences	Misleading prejudgment	Self-interest	Attach-ment	Comments and other
Based on public data (continued)					
14. Enron—special-purpose vehicles	Some	Some	Major	—	
15. Mattel—brand extension	Major	Major	—	—	
16. Battle of Arnhem	Some	Major	Major	Some	
17. Essilor—new technology	Major	Major	Limited	Some	
18. Inchcape—acquisition of TKM	?	Some	Some	Some	
19. Disguised case—new technology	?	Some	Limited	Major	
20. Courtaulds—new thread	Limited	Some	Some	Major	
21. ImClone—commercialize new cancer drug	Some	Some	Major	Some	
22. Xerox—office automation	—	Major	Some	—	
23. M&S—acquisition of Brooks Brothers	—	Some	—	Major	
24. Home Depot—restructuring	Major	Some	Some	—	
25. Oracle—acquisition of PeopleSoft	—	—	Some	Major	
26. Paul Wolfowitz—package for his partner	—	?	—	Major	
27. Samsung—entry into cars	Some	Some	—	Major	
28. West Virginia University—MBA award	—	Some	Some	Some	
29. Hurricane Katrina—Broderick's decision on levee breaches	Major	Major	—	?	
30. Bay of Pigs	—	Major	Some	—	
31. Coca-Cola—Belgian product contamination	Some	Limited	Major	—	
32. Encyclopedia Britannica—electronic products	Major	Major	Some	Some	
33. Firestone-Bridgestone merger	Major	Some	—	—	
34. Food Lion—expansion strategy	Major	Some	—	—	
Number of "major"	35	44	25	15	
Number of "some"	18	24	32	21	
Total	53	68	57	36	
As % of total cases					
"Major"	42%	53%	30%	18%	
"Some"	22%	29%	39%	25%	
Total "major" and "some"	64%	82%	69%	43%	

Database of Safeguards

I N THIS APPENDIX we provide checklists to help you generate ideas for safeguards or cross-check that good ideas have not been over-looked. The structure used is that in the main text, where safeguards were divided into four categories (see figure AII-1). We also comment on some other potential safeguards and their limitations. Further ideas are available on our Web site.

FIGURE AII-1

Four types of safeguard

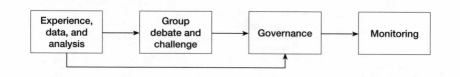

Experience, Data, and Analysis

One way to safeguard against a flawed decision is to bring in new experience, data, and analysis (see figure AII-2). The aim is to provide the decision maker with new patterns and emotional tags—thus addressing any potential distortions in their thinking at the source.

Experience, data, and analysis checklist

Type of safeguard	Examples
Expose decision makers to new experiences	• Organize customer visits, days in the field • Allocate information-collecting roles to executives—e.g., R&D, marketing • Share information about the industry on a regular basis[a] • Increase the flow of real-time information to executives[b]
Appoint advisers who have different experiences from those of the decision makers	• Use internal experts or people from diverse parts of the organization[c] for particular analytical modules • Do interviews with external experts, people with other experience • Use outside consultants with specialist expertise
Buy in data and analysis	• Purchase or commission industry reports and studies • Use case studies, industry analogies, or analogies with other decisions,[d] industry life-cycle analysis, and patterns from others' experience[e]
Do analysis of key assumptions	• Focus analysis on specific elements of the classical decision process—e.g., create alternative frames for the problem, lay out the link between the frame and the criteria, identify potential options, discuss the key assumptions, create detailed implementation • Do extra modules of analysis on key areas of uncertainty, particularly where experience about these uncertainties is limited—e.g., test key assumptions, evaluate risk/return trade-offs between different options • Do extra modules of analysis for areas where there are apparently anomalous results—e.g., analyze the potential meanings of weak signals • Pressure test the proposed solution—e.g., adding 25% to the downside case • Create a simulation to model the consequences of particular choices
Use provocative data and analysis to challenge strongly held prejudgments or other powerful emotional tags	• Ask decision makers to list weaknesses in their argument[f] • Use very compelling and counterintuitive analogies or case studies to challenge key assumptions • Adopt a "blank sheet of paper" approach, starting with the framing and the selection of options • Commission provocative studies by an individual or a group that does not share the emotional connections to members of the group—e.g., to evaluate second-choice options[g] • Use "frame breaking" techniques such as scenario analysis to challenge existing views of the situation, or gaming to challenge how a range of options might turn out[h] • Make decision makers analyze how a competitor or start-up might attack their business, so that they think of different frames or options • Run competitive games/war games involving decision makers

a. Kathleen M. Eisenhardt, "Strategy as Strategic Decision Making," *Sloan Management Review* 40, no. 3 (Spring 1999)
b. Ibid.
c. John T. Horn, Dan P. Lovallo, and S. Patrick Viguerie, "Beating the Odds in Market Entry," *McKinsey Quarterly*, no. 4 (2005)
d. Ibid.
e. Ibid.
f. Linda Babcock and George Loewenstein, "Explaining Bargaining Impasse: The Role of Self-Serving Bias," *Journal of Economic Perspectives* 11, no. 1 (1997), 115--116.
g. Dan P. Lovallo and Olivier Sibony, "Distortions and Deceptions in Strategic Decisions," *McKinsey Quarterly*, no. 1 (2006)
h. Eisenhardt, "Strategy as Strategic Decision Making."

Group Debate and Challenge

Putting together a carefully chosen group of people to debate a decision is one of the most useful ways of reducing the risk of a flawed decision. Data and analysis are most likely to influence the already open mind, whereas a well-chosen decision group is more likely to ensure that assumptions are fully challenged, options rigorously debated, and biases exposed.

Fortunately, there is a vast amount of advice on how to select the right group and ensure that people speak up. Broadly speaking, the two approaches available are to change either the membership of the decision group or the design of the decision-making process—but there are many variants, some of which are listed in figure AII-3.

FIGURE AII-3

Group debate and challenge checklist

Type of safeguard	Examples
Pool experience to identify and stimulate a range of viewpoints	• Go around the table, asking each member of the group to give their views and/or express their doubts • Hold meetings at which different viewpoints are shared on key uncertainties involved in the decision—e.g., the attractiveness of the market, sources of competitive advantage, nature of the environment, competitor threats • Hold meetings to discuss elements of the classical decision process—e.g., framing, options, judgments, or implementation challenges[a] • Brainstorm frames, options, criteria, etc. • Add a facilitator • Change the group process to create new dynamics and discussion—e.g., change from formal to informal, or from informal to formal, or from integrated discussion into two or more separate groups[b] • Minimize status/rank differences and protocol,[c] improve group cohesiveness,[d] increase psychological safety[e] to make group members more comfortable challenging general wisdom or strong members of the group
Add new members who have different viewpoints	• Put an internal expert or external consultant on the decision team • Add people with different personal interests[f] and/or emotional tags—e.g., skeptical generalists,[g] managers with a different business background, managers from other businesses, or board members • Add the implementer to the decision group • Increase the communication to and from the decision group to increase the diversity of viewpoints and consequent challenge[h] • Or the opposite: remove "problem" members of the group

(continued)

FIGURE AII-3 *(continued)*

Group debate and challenge checklist

Type of safeguard	Examples
Directly challenge decision makers to reflect on their emotional tags	• Lay out outcomes in more "objective" terms that can be compared with each other—e.g., NPV, risk/return comparisons, with assumptions highlighted • Create pairings of senior decision makers with complementary patterns and emotional tags • Use a confidential adviser to listen to, advise, and challenge senior decision makers[i]—e.g., chairman or board member; a favored consultant, investment banker, or personal coach; an HR person; a trusted insider; or a member of the kitchen cabinet • Conduct some training and exercises in decision-making traps

Customize roles and goals to encourage new and appropriate viewpoints	• Assign individuals or subgroups different roles in the decision process—e.g.:
	  • Split the authorizer, evaluator, and proposer roles
	  • Use the RAPID approach—i.e., allocate decision responsibilities: recommend, agree, perform, input, decide[j]
	  • Allocate de Bono's "hats"[k]
	  • Define ad hoc roles as needed—e.g., futurist, steadying force, action orientation
	• Create customized role-playing
	• Establish common goals for the group and the decision process[l]
	• Ask managers to analyze what they would do if they owned the business

Design the decision process to encourage conflict between people with different viewpoints	• Have a session to identify new frames, options, criteria • Add process steps in which challenge to the prevailing wisdom is solicited • Collect group members' opinions privately—e.g., through interview or a questionnaire; then review the findings in the group • Do a survey or e-mail a structured questionnaire to a sample of people outside the decision group to get their view on options, etc. • Use secret voting or similar voting approaches to flush out different opinions • Use an external facilitator or chairman to ensure that challenges are identified and nurtured • Use formal approaches that increase challenge in a structured way—e.g., dialectical inquiry (asking a separate group to present an alternative option, then having the whole group work together to identify the best option), devil's advocate process (a subgroup attacks the proposed option)[m] • Ensure there is a divergent phase in which new options are generated;[n] require multiple options to be identified and analyzed[o] • Conduct a before-the-fact postmortem on the decision, as if it had failed • Communicate openness to challenge through the personal behaviors of the leader and most senior members of the group

a. Kathleen M. Eisenhardt, "Strategy as Strategic Decision Making," *Sloan Management Review* 40, no. 3 (Spring 1999).
b. Michael A. Roberto, *Why Great Leaders Don't Take Yes for an Answer: Managing for Conflict and Consensus.* (Upper Saddle River, NJ: Wharton School Publishing, 2005), 43–44.
c. Ibid. page, 32.
d. John Hunt, interview with author.
e. Roberto, *Why Great Leaders Don't Take Yes for an Answer*, 42, quoting Amy Edmondson.
f. Eisenhardt, "Strategy as Strategic Decision Making."
g. Roberto, *Why Great Leaders Don't Take Yes for an Answer*, 32.

(continued)

FIGURE AII-3 *(continued)*

Group debate and challenge checklist

h. Ibid., 62.

i. Ibid., 38.

j. Paul Rogers and Marcia Blenko, "Who Has the D? How Clear Decision Roles Enhance Organizational Performance," *Harvard Business Review*, January 2006.

k. Edward de Bono, *Six Thinking Hats* (Boston: Little, Brown, 1985).

l. Eisenhardt, "Strategy as Strategic Decision Making."

m. Roberto, *Why Great Leaders Don't Take Yes for an Answer*, 52.

n. Thomas M. Scheidel, "Divergent and Convergent Thinking in Group Decision-Making," in *Communication and Group Decision-Making*, eds. Randy Y. Hirokawa and Marshall Scott Poole (Beverly Hills, CA: Sage Publications, 1986); and T. S. Kuhn, "The Essential Tension: Tradition and Innovation in Scientific Research," in *Scientific Creativity*, eds. Calvin W. Taylor and Frank Barron (New York: John Wiley, 1963).

o. Roberto, *Why Great Leaders Don't Take Yes for an Answer*, 32; Dan P. Lovallo and Olivier Sibony, "Distortions and Deceptions in Strategic Decisions," *McKinsey Quarterly*, no. 1 (2006); and Eisenhardt, "Strategy as Strategic Decision Making."

Governance

The governance process (see figure AII-4) can be the strongest form of safeguard—particularly when the decision team leader is also a strong champion of the proposed option, a common situation in large organizations.

FIGURE AII-4

Governance checklist

Type of safeguard	Examples
Add individuals to the governance process	• Add an individual with relevant expertise in the uncertainties concerned—e.g., international markets, implementation requirements • Add an individual with different emotional connections—e.g., different prejudgments, no attachments to the status quo
Call for extra data and analysis	• Request further data and analysis to supplement that provided normally by the decision group • Use or build links to people in the organization who can provide background information and opinions • Commission an independent review • Ask challenging questions
Strengthen the governance process to add challenge	• Create a subcommittee to preview the proposal • Increase the time spent debating aspects of the decision—e.g., business background, framing, options, criteria • Add extra layers of governance—e.g., more reviews, meetings with other stakeholders • Require that the decision be brought back for review at particular stage gates

(continued)

FIGURE AII-4 (*continued*)

Governance checklist

Type of safeguard	Examples
Review and modify the overall decision process	• Advise on, or ask for a report on, the decision group and process used • Create a checklist of potential red flags, and suggest appropriate safeguards • Have a member of the governance team sit as a "fly on the wall" in the decision process
Test for commitment	• Adopt an aggressive, challenging style • Turn down the decision—initially

Note: It is also possible to use many of the safeguards described in the group debate and challenge checklist (Fig. AII-3) to strengthen the governamce process.

Monitoring

If all else fails, the monitoring process (see figure AII-5) can be used to reduce the risk of flawed decisions.

FIGURE AII-5

Monitoring checklist

Type of safeguard	Examples
Test commitment by preannouncing a monitoring process	• Clarify the measures of performance • Establish a postaudit process for all major decisions • Announce a special postaudit or reporting for a particular decision • Link results of the decision directly to compensation and other rewards
Set up a formal review process and adjust the decision according to the results	• Require a prototype or trial, and set performance requirements • Use gated funding—e.g., as in drug companies
Improve the ability to respond during implementation to emerging results	• Install a strong implementation team • Improve the ability to learn and be flexible during implementation • Build in more optionality to the outcome[a]

a. Charles Roxburgh, "Hidden Flaws in Strategy," *McKinsey Quarterly*, no. 2 (2003).

One Other Type of Safeguard: Organizational and Environmental Context

We should briefly mention one other type of potential safeguard—and the reason why we have not included it in this book (although it is described more on our Web site).

The *organizational and environmental context* influences decision makers. For example, one of the authors interviewed a CEO and a finance director of a gas meter manufacturer that was strongly focused on maximizing return on capital. Their pretax return on capital was in excess of 35 percent, and they rightly felt proud of their performance. The author asked whether they would be prepared to invest in an opportunity offering 20 or 25 percent returns—thus depressing their average return. The management team admitted that that would be difficult to do—even though they agreed with the author that those returns would be well above the cost of capital.

The limitation of the organizational and environmental context as a safeguard is that in most cases it is not practical to change it in the time frame of the decision. For this reason, we have not covered it further in this book. However, changes in the context may well be a powerful way of improving a series of decisions and the overall quality of decision making in the longer term. Some elements of context are described in figure AII-6.

FIGURE AII-6

Context checklist

Type of safeguard	Examples
Overall roles, metrics, reward systems	• Job descriptions and role definitions • Explicit and implicit performance measures • Bonus structure • Promotion criteria
Structure and hierarchy	• Communication flows up, down, and across the organization • Willingness to challenge superiors
Systems and processes	• Budgeting • Capital allocation and spending approval • Strategy • Target setting • Performance review
Strategy	• Type of strategy—e.g., growth, cost reduction • Recent or notable strategic successes or failures
Decision-making culture	• Intuitive versus analytical • Action versus planning oriented • Decision-making style—role models provided by "heroes and icons" • Shared values • Training and development programs
Important stakeholders	• Major shareholders, owners • Customers, suppliers • Others—e.g., trade associations, unions
External influences	• Industry recipes • Recent success stories from competitors

NOTES

Chapter 1

1. Christopher Cooper and Robert Block, *Disaster: Hurricane Katrina and the Failure of Homeland Security* (New York: Time Books, 2006), 100.
2. http://www.usnews.com/usnews/news/articles/060303/3dhs.htm.
3. U.S. Congress, Senate Committee on Homeland Security and Governmental Affairs, Special Investigation of the Hurricane Katrina Response, *Interview of Matthew Broderick*, 2006, 110.
4. Ibid., 14.
5. Ibid., 70.
6. U.S. Congress, Senate Committee on Homeland Security and Governmental Affairs, *Hurricane Katrina: The Roles of DHS and FEMA Leadership*, February 10, 2006, 206–210.
7. Ibid., 210.
8. U.S. Congress, *Interview of Matthew Broderick*, 86.
9. Cooper and Block, *Disaster*, 159.
10. U.S. Congress, *Interview of Matthew Broderick*, 47.
11. Cooper and Block, *Disaster*, 164.
12. V. S. Ramachandran and Sandra Blakeslee, *Phantoms in the Brain: Human Nature and the Architecture of the Mind* (London: Fourth Estate, 1998), 72.

Chapter 2

1. William D. Smithburg, interview by author, January 18, 2001.
2. Greg Prince, "Come Together," *Beverage World*, December 1995, 50–54.
3. Smithburg interview.
4. Interviews with Michael Weinstein, former CEO, Triarc Beverage Group, in Sydney Finkelstein, *Why Smart Executives Fail and What You Can Learn from their Mistakes* (New York: Portfolio, 2003).
5. V. S. Ramachandran and Sandra Blakeslee, *Phantoms in the Brain: Human Nature and the Architecture of the Mind* (London: Fourth Estate, 1998), 110.
6. Ibid., 238.
7. Ibid., 64. The original case, including this incident, is reported in A. D. Milner et al., "Perception and Action in 'Visual Form Agnosia,'" *Brain* 114 (1991).
8. Milner et al., "Perception and Action in 'Visual Form Agnosia.'"
9. Specifically in this case, Ramachandran suggests that there are many parts of the brain involved in vision, some of which operate at a subconscious level. These may act as

quick triggers, alerting our conscious brain to things that we need to examine in more detail, such as a charging mammoth or an incoming missile. There may also be triggers allowing us to take quick, reflexive action such as ducking, flinching, or pumping out adrenalin. These "zombies" may follow an "older" pathway in the brain via the brain stem, which is a part of the brain shared by more primitive animals such as reptiles. They may, therefore, be reflex responses inherited from our evolutionary past. Ramachandran describes this as "blind sight." In the case of Diane, the explanation is more complex. Even in that part of our vision that is more recently evolved, there is a split between what Ramachandran describes as the "What" pathway and the "How." The What pathway tells us what an object is and is associated with the temporal lobe of the brain; the How pathway helps with spatial awareness and is associated with the parietal lobe. Diane had suffered damage to the What but not the How pathway—so that she new *how* to reach the pencil, although she could not see *what* it was. The general point that this example illustrates is the degree to which we are not fully conscious of all that is going on in our brains when we sense the world and respond by making decisions.

10. A good book on the speed with which we can form judgments is Malcolm Gladwell's highly readable *Blink: The Power of Thinking Without Thinking* (London: Penguin, 2006).

11. Robert J. Sternberg, *Why Smart People Can Be so Stupid* (New Haven & London: Yale University Press, 2002).

12. For those interested in more dramatic examples of experience being a deceptive guide, Ramachandran describes a number of types of patients who imagined things based on past experience. People who have lost a limb imagine the limb to still be there. People who suffer a scomata (a brain injury that causes them to lose a part of their vision) will hallucinate in the area where they cannot see, seeking to fill the gap with something based on their experience; but these things can be very weird—e.g., cartoons, monkeys, Hawaiian dancers. Patients suffering from this know that what they see cannot be true—but it still seems real to them.

13. Ramachandran and Blakeslee, *Phantoms in the Brain*.

Chapter 3

1. Charles Kenney, *Riding the Runaway Horse: The Rise and Decline of Wang Laboratories* (Boston: Little, Brown & Company, 1992), 48, 165–167.

2. For example, Ken Olsen, founder of Digital Equipment Corporation, famously said in 1977, "There is no reason for any individual to have a personal computer in his home."

3. Martin Middlebrook, *Arnhem 1944* (London: Viking, 1994), 66.

4. Norman Dixon, *On the Psychology of Military Incompetence* (London: Pimlico, Random House, 1994), 147.

5. Max Hastings, *Armageddon: The Battle for Germany, 1944–1945* (London: Pan Macmillan, 2006), 66.

6. Dixon, *On the Psychology of Military Incompetence*, 168.

7. Hastings, *Armageddon*, 39.

8. Ibid., 40.

9. Ibid.

10. Antoine Bechara et al., "Insensitivity to Future Consequences Following Damage to Human Prefrontal Cortex," *Cognition* 50, no. 1-3 (1994): 7–15.

11. Antoine Bechara, Hanna Damasio, and Antonio Damasio, "Emotion, Decision Making and the Orbitofrontal Cortex," *Cerebral Cortex* 10, no. 3 (2000): 295–307.

12. Antonio Damasio, *Looking for Spinoza: Joy, Sorrow and the Feeling Brain* (London: Vintage, 2004), 147.

13. Ibid., 148.

14. Antonio Damasio, *Descartes' Error: Emotion, Reason, and the Human Brain* (New York: Grosset/Putnam, 1994).

15. Research has also been done with patients who had damage to the amygdala. These patients did not experience an emotional reaction to the negative cards and were more likely to continue picking from the bad decks. Nasir Naqvi, Baba Shiv, and Antoine Bechara, "The Role of Emotion in Decision Making," *Current Directions in Psychological Science* 15, no. 5 (2006).

16. Daniel Goleman, *Emotional Intelligence: Why It Can Matter More Than IQ*, 10th anniversary reissue ed. (New York: Bantam Books, 2006).

17. Damasio suggests that the memories and associated emotions may be stored in different parts of the brain, but that the ventromedial prefrontal cortex (a part of our cerebral cortex, also called the orbitofrontal cortex because of its position just above the eyes) acts as a link between them. In his words, "Structures in the ventromedial prefrontal cortex provide the substrate for learning an association between certain classes of complex situation, on the one hand, and the type of bioregulatory state (including emotional state) usually associated with that class of situation in past individual experience. The ventromedial sector holds linkages between the facts that compose a given situation, and the emotion previously paired with it in an individual's contingent experience." Bechara, Damasio, and Damasio, "Emotion, Decision Making and the Orbitofrontal Cortex," 296. In consequence, past memories and their associated emotions become linked together—memories are tagged with their associated emotions. This process of emotional tagging is part of what Damasio refers to as the *somatic-marker hypothesis*.

18. For further discussion, see Michael A. Roberto, *Why Great Leaders Don't Take Yes for an Answer: Managing for Conflict and Consensus* (Upper Saddle River, NJ: Wharton School Publishing, 2005).

19. Damasio, *Descartes' Error*, 193.

20. For more discussion of this in the context of Montgomery and military leaders, see Dixon, *On the Psychology of Military Incompetence*, 164–166. The original theory of cognitive dissonance is associated with Leon Festinger; see Leon Festinger, *A Theory of Cognitive Dissonance* (Evanston, IL: Row Peterson, 1957) and is discussed further in Chapter 6.

21. Note that there are not clear physical boundaries between these systems (in that respect, the diagram in figure 3-1 is an oversimplification). Rather, MacLean's idea is that the brain can be imagined as consisting of three different systems that work alongside each other but at very different levels of consciousness, with different purposes and different ways of operating. So, for example, emotions operate on decision making in a very different way from reason. For a defense of MacLean's theory, see Gerald A. Cory Jr., *The Reciprocal Modular Brain in Economics and Politics: Shaping the Rational and Moral Basis of Organization, Exchange, and Choice* (New York: Kluwer Academic/Plenum Publishers, 1999).

22. Goleman, *Emotional Intelligence*, 289.

23. Colin Camerer, George Loewenstein, and Drazan Prelec, "Neuroeconomics: How Neuroscience Can Inform Economics," *Journal of Economic Literature* 43, no. 1 (2005): 9–64.

24. Goleman, *Emotional Intelligence*, 291.

25. Described in Joseph LeDoux, *The Emotional Brain* (London: Phoenix, in association with Simon & Schuster, 1999), 59; quoting a meta-analysis by Bornstein and experiments by Zajonc.

26. Goleman, *Emotional Intelligence*, 28.

27. Laurence Gonzales, *Deep Survival: Who Lives, Who Dies and Why* (New York: W. W. Norton, 2003).

28. Ibid., 33.

29. LeDoux, *The Emotional Brain*.

30. Naqvi, Shiv, and Bechara explain the involuntary nature of emotions elegantly: "As each option is brought to mind, the somatic state that was triggered by that behaviour in the past is re-enacted by the ventromedial prefrontal cortex. After the emotional states are elicited in the body, during decision making, they are represented in the brain through a sensory process. This can occur in two ways. The mapping of bodily states at the cortical level . . . gives rise to 'gut feelings' of desire or aversion that are attributed to specific behavioural

options. The mapping of bodily states at the subcortical level . . . occurs in a non-conscious fashion, such that subjects choose the advantageous option without feeling specific feelings of desire for that option or aversion to the disadvantageous option." Naqvi, Shiv, and Bechara, "The Role of Emotion in Decision Making."

Chapter 4

1. Our understanding of this decision comes mainly from Jonathan Parshall and Anthony Tully, *Shattered Sword: The Untold Story of the Battle of Midway* (Washington, DC: Potomac Books, 2005).

2. Gary Klein, *Sources of Power: How People Make Decisions* (Cambridge, MA: MIT Press, 1999).

3. Recent research by Ap Dijksterhuis, professor of psychology at Amsterdam University, has demonstrated the effectiveness of our unconscious decision making. Ap Dijksterhuis and Loran F. Nordgren, "A Theory of Unconscious Thought," *Perspectives on Psychological Science* 1, no. 2 (2006).

4. E.g., Erving Goffman, *Frame Analysis: An Essay on the Organization of Experience* (London: Harper & Row, 1974).

5. A question of interest concerns why we have evolved a one-plan-at-a-time decision process. Herbert Simon, who won the Nobel Prize in economics in 1978 for his pioneering research into the decision-making process within economic organizations, was the first to observe that we typically conduct only a limited search for alternatives when making decisions. His explanation was that we suffer from *bounded rationality*. In Simon's view, we are unable to be fully rational because we have a limited capacity to process information. Because of constraints to the size of our working memories, we use a one-plan-at-a-time process because we do not have the mental capacity to consider multiple options at the same time. Herbert Simon called this behavior "satisficing." Herbert A. Simon, *Models of Bounded Rationality*, 3 vols. (Cambridge, MA: MIT Press, 1982).

Klein's research suggests that the reason we use the one-plan-at-a-time process may be because, in most situations, it is a superior way to make decisions. We may have evolved this way of making decisions because it enabled us to survive better than those humans and prehumans who were evolving a different approach to decision making. Klein's firefighters, after all, were able to make snap decisions that saved lives, based on limited information. Gonzales's pilots can, with a few exceptions, successfully land a fighter jet on an aircraft carrier in the toughest of weather conditions. The one-plan-at-a-time process is both effective and efficient when we are sufficiently expert in the conditions we are facing.

Chapter 5

1. All Sir Clive Thompson quotes in this chapter are from interviews with author.

2. Amos Tversky and Daniel Kahneman, "Availability: A Heuristic for Judging Frequency and Probability," *Cognitive Psychology* 5, no. 2 (1973).

3. Amos Tversky and Daniel Kahneman, "Judgment Under Uncertainty: Heuristics and Biases," *Science* 185, no. 4157 (1974). Discussed in Max H. Bazerman, *Judgment in Managerial Decision Making*, 6th ed. (Hoboken, NJ: Wiley, 2006), 18, 19.

4. Bazerman, *Judgment in Managerial Decision Making*, 18–21.

5. Daniel Kahneman and Amos Tversky, "On the Psychology of Prediction," *Psychological Review* 80 (1973). Discussed in Bazerman, *Judgment in Managerial Decision Making*, 9, 21–29.

6. Research has shown that when information is presented in a way that allows people to relate it to their own experience, it is much more likely that they will be able to make good decisions. For example, Gerd Gigerenzer and his research partners designed an experiment in which they asked doctors the same problem but in two different ways. In the first, they posed a problem in terms of probability theory:

- One percent of women have breast cancer

- If a woman has breast cancer, then she has an 80% chance of having a positive mammogram.

- If the woman does not have breast cancer, the probability is 10% that she will still have a positive mammogram.

- What is the probability that a woman with a positive mammogram has breast cancer?

The doctors did badly. Only two out of twenty came up with the right answer. The median estimate by the doctors was 70%. The correct answer is 7.5%.

However, doctors are not experienced in thinking about probabilities. When the same problem is expressed in a more familiar way—one that is more likely to have links with past decisions the doctors have made—they do much better. So Gigerenzer repeated the experiment, using frequencies:

- Ten out of 1,000 women have breast cancer.

- Of these 10, 8 will have a positive mammogram.

- Of the remaining 990 women who do not have breast cancer, 99 will still have a positive mammogram.

- How many of a sample of 100 women with a positive mammogram will actually have breast cancer?

As a result of this simple reframing of the problem, sixteen out of twenty-four doctors got the answer right. (See G. Gigerenzer, *Adaptive Thinking: Rationality in the Real World* (New York: Oxford University Press, 2000).

Gigerenzer argues that expressing the data in terms of natural frequencies rather than probabilities produced better results because this more closely matches our experience—doctors have seen a lot of patients who have had positive tests and understand that a proportion of them will not go on to develop a disease, but they have not "seen" or experienced a probability. Gerd Gigerenzer, *Adaptive Thinking: Rationality in the Real World* (New York: Oxford University Press, 2000), 65–67.

7. Another way to identify potentially misleading experiences is to think about the *types* of experience rather than the *sources* of the experience. The main types of experience to consider are based on the one-plan-at-a-time process that our brain uses to make decisions, as described in chapter 4:

- *Misleading experiences about the situation.* Thompson's experience was that acquisitions offered the opportunity for gain rather than loss, and that they offered the best way to grow at 20 percent per year. The main challenge was to close the deal at a reasonable premium to current value. He did not see the downside.

- *Misleading experiences about options.* Thompson did not seem to have any misleading experience about the options.

- *Misleading experiences about objectives and criteria.* Thompson may not have fully appreciated the risks involved in the deal. His past experience had suggested that the risks were manageable and were therefore not important criteria to consider.

- *Misleading experiences about abilities.* Thompson had misleading experiences that led him to believe he had the ability to get value out of all new acquisitions. If there was a problem he had enough depth in his team to pour management resources in, turn the business around, and integrate it into the

Rentokil culture. Unfortunately, the size of BET and Securigard made this experience misleading.

- *Misleading experiences about likely outcomes.* Rentokil's experience and the example of Granada suggested that acquisitions were generally highly successful.

We find that thinking about the sources of misleading experience is a more direct way to identify them—particularly if the decision is a strategic decision. However, this second approach is useful as an alternative, complement. or cross-check.

Chapter 6

1. Steve Russell, interview by author.

2. Because prejudgments are often judgments we have distilled from previous experiences, this red flag is closely associated with the red flag of misleading experiences. The difference is that in the case of a prejudgment, a previous experience has received a particularly strong emotional tag because the decision maker has made a decision or judgment as a result of the experience. Prejudgments can also arise from attachments—for example, a prejudgment that closing a particular company would be a mistake. While prejudgments are not wholly independent of some of the other red flags (they draw on the common root of patterns and emotions), there is considerable research demonstrating the strong biases resulting from the way the human brain can become anchored to judgments it has made. So we wanted to be sure to highlight prejudgments to ensure that adequate attention is given to this well-documented aspect of the way our brains work.

3. John Kenneth Galbraith, *The Great Crash, 1929* (London: Penguin Books, 1992).

4. Robert J. Sternberg, *Why Smart People Can Be so Stupid* (New Haven & London: Yale University Press, 2002).

5. Ibid.

6. Leon Festinger, *A Theory of Cognitive Dissonance* (Evanston, IL: Row Peterson, 1957).

7. E.g., for a general discussion, see Max H. Bazerman, *Judgment in Managerial Decision Making*, 6th ed. (Hoboken, NJ: Wiley, 2006).

8. Dan Ariely, George Loewenstein, and Drazan Prelec, "Determinants of Anchoring Effects," unpublished manuscript (2000).

9. Amos Tversky and Daniel Kahneman, "Judgment Under Uncertainty: Heuristics and Biases," *Science* 185, no. 4157 (1974).

10. Thomas Mussweiler and Fritz Strack, "Hypothesis-Consistent Testing and Semantic Priming in the Anchoring Paradigm: A Selective Accessibility Model," *Journal of Experimental Social Psychology* 35, no. 2 (1999). Described in Bazerman, *Judgment in Managerial Decision Making*, 29.

11. Bazerman, *Judgment in Managerial Decision Making*.

12. V. S. Ramachandran and Sandra Blakeslee, *Phantoms in the Brain: Human Nature and the Architecture of the Mind* (London: Fourth Estate, 1998), 136.

13. Ibid.

14. Note that we describe prejudgments by *type* rather than by *source*. The alert reader will remember that we described misleading experiences by source rather than type, leaving our alternative description by type to the endnotes. The difference in our approach is that because there are so many potential sources of prejudgments we find it counterproductive to go through them all. Therefore we list them by type. Whereas we had three sources of misleading experience, potential sources of prejudgments include many others. For example, sources of prejudgments we have observed include:

- *Prejudgments from the three sources of misleading experience described in chapter 5.* Misleading experiences can sometimes be the basis for prejudgments.

Judgments formed on the basis of experience receive strong and positive emotional tags. Over time these may strengthen. President Hoover, and decision makers for decades before, had been brought up observing that those who got into debt could end up in the poorhouse. As another example, Wallace became anchored on his trust in mediums partly because he had experienced the materialization of a six-foot sunflower during a séance.

- *Prejudgments from the views of other stakeholders.* Thompson may have developed a prejudgment that he had to try and keep growing the earnings of Rentokil by 20 percent a year because shareholders were pressing him to do so and his management team was looking for additional "raw meat."

- *Prejudgments from commitments already made—particularly public ones.* Prior to his developing and implementing the strategy, Russell had been quite clear about his intended strategy of growing Boots presence in healthcare markets. His commitment to this growth strategy may have strengthened his conviction in this prejudgment.

- *Prejudgments from industry recipes and popular strategies.* Wallace's fixation on mediums came at a time when many people had a great interest in spirits and mediums. Lloyds' (a large U.K. retail bank) problematic acquisition of Scottish Widows (a U.K. life insurance company) came at a time when the idea of "bancassurance"— the cross selling of insurance products to bank customers was widely accepted as an attractive growth strategy.

- *Prejudgments from a desire to lead and commit to action.* For example, Russell's prejudgment that healthcare services were the right way to go was probably strengthened as he tried to motivate those around him to make it a success.

- *Prejudgments from trusted advisors and confidants.* Gurus can often cause those who employ them to make disastrous decisions.

- *. . . and no doubt there are others.*

Another issue with trying to identify prejudgments by considering their source is that many prejudgments seem to have arisen in the murky past and, by the time of the decision, have an uncertain source. This means that trying to identify prejudgments by thinking about their source can be a frustrating and fruitless exercise. Better to just consider what prejudgments the decision maker has. For example, it would have been clear to those around him that Russell had a prejudgment to go into healthcare services, but not clear what the true source of this was. But it is not necessary to know the original source of the prejudgment to identify it!

15. Steve Russell, interview by author.

Chapter 7

1. Bill Saporito, "How Fastow Helped Enron Fall," *Time*, 2002, www.time.com/time/business/article/0 percent2C8599 percent2C201871 percent2C00.html.

2. Robert Bryce, *Pipe Dreams* (New York: Public Affairs, 2002), 248. Note: twenty-eight executives and board members made $1.2 billion from exercising their stock options between 1998 and 2001.

3. Wikipedia, "Enron," http://en.wikipedia.org/wiki/Enron.

4. By *self-interest* we mean the mix of personal interests that a decision maker has (at the end of the chapter, we give a list of the most common types of interest). For there to be inappropriate self-interest, two conditions must apply. First, there must be a differential impact on these interests, depending on which option is selected. Second, the impact on the

decision maker's interests must be different in direction (positive or negative) and/or magnitude from the impact on the other legitimate stakeholders involved in the decision (to avoid a long digression, we leave a definition of *legitimate* to the reader). Clearly, the degree of "conflict" between the interests of the decision maker and other stakeholders can vary from decision to decision.

5. Stephen Budiansky, Ted Gest, and David Fischer, "How Lawyers Abuse the Law," *US News and World Report*, January 30, 1995. Reported in Max H. Bazerman, *Judgment in Managerial Decision Making*, 6th ed. (Hoboken, NJ: Wiley, 2006), 74.

6. Bazerman, *Judgment in Managerial Decision Making*. The results of this experiment may explain why Enron's auditors failed to flag to shareholders that Enron's accounts were not a fair reflection of the financial health of the company. Arthur Andersen, the auditor, approved Enron's accounts even though it knew that they contained irregularities. The Arthur Andersen partners in charge of the Enron account benefited personally from the high value of their relationship with Enron, and stood to lose significantly if Enron's management decided not to reemploy them. Enron paid Arthur Andersen $52 million in fees in 2000, and fees were expected to rise to $100 million soon thereafter; reported in Susan E. Squires et al., *Inside Arthur Andersen: Shifting Values, Unexpected Consequences* (Upper Saddle River, NJ: FT Prentice Hall, 2003), 21.

7. Squires et al., *Inside Arthur Andersen*.

8. Jeffrey Peppercorn et al., "Association Between Pharmaceutical Involvement and Outcomes in Breast Cancer Clinical Trials," *Cancer* 109, no. 7 (2007).

9. Anne Underwood, "Too Good to Be True?" *Newsweek Online*, February 26, 2007.

10. Dan Ariely, *Predictably Irrational: The Hidden Forces That Shape Our Decisions* (London: HarperCollins, 2008).

11. Specifically: "The distribution of the number of correctly solved questions remained the same across all four conditions, but with a mean shift when the participants could cheat." Ibid.

12. George Loewenstein et al., "Self-Serving Assessments of Fairness and Pretrial Bargaining," *Journal of Legal Studies* 22, no. 1 (1993).

13. Linda Babcock, George Loewenstein, and Samuel Issacharoff, "Creating Convergence: Debiasing Biased Litigants," *Law Society Inquiry* 22 (1997).

14. Jason Dana and George Loewenstein, "A Social Science Perspective on Gifts to Physicians from Industry," *JAMA* 290, no. 2 (2003).

15. Linda Babcock and George Loewenstein, "Explaining Bargaining Impasse: The Role of Self-Serving Bias," *Journal of Economic Perspectives* 11, no. 1 (1997).

16. In a separate paper, Moore and Loewenstein summarize a more general body of evidence on the effects of self-interest by concluding "that the violations of professionalism induced by conflicts of interest often occur automatically and without conscious awareness." Don Moore and George Loewenstein, "Self-Interest, Automaticity, and the Psychology of Conflict of Interest," *Social Justice Research* 17, no. 2 (2004).

17. Dana and Loewenstein, "A Social Science Perspective."

18. Eugene M. Caruso, Nicholas Epley, and Max H. Bazerman, "The Good, the Bad and the Ugly of Perspective Taking in Groups," in *Research on Managing Groups and Teams: Ethics and Groups*, eds. Elizabeth A. Mannix, Margaret A. Neale, and Ann E. Tenbrunsel (New York: Elsevier/JAI, 2005); and Seale Harris, *Banting's Miracle: The Story of the Discovery of Insulin* (Toronto: J. M. Dent & Sons, 1946). Discussed in Bazerman, *Judgment in Managerial Decision Making*, 123–124.

19. Michael Ross and Fiore Sicoly, "Moral Ambiguity, Moral Constraints, and Self-Serving Biases," *Journal of Personality and Social Psychology* 37, no. 3 (1979).

20. More precisely, part of our brain retains the knowledge that we have not been fair, as knowing the truth is helpful, but our conscious mind is persuaded that we have been fair. E.g., see Steven Pinker, *How the Mind Works* (London: Penguin Books, 1999), 421.

21. E.g., see Pinker, *How the Mind Works*.

22. Linda Babcock et al., "Biased Judgments for Fairness in Bargaining," *American Economic Review* 85, no. 5 (1995): 1342.

23. Babcock and Loewenstein, "Explaining Bargaining Impasse."

24. Roderick M. Kramer, "Self-Enhancing Cognitions and Organizational Conflict," working paper (1994); and Robert Sutton and Roderick M. Kramer, "Transforming Failure into Success: Impression Management, the Reagan Administration, and the Iceland Arms Control Talks," in *Organizations and Nation-States: New Perspectives on Conflict and Cooperation*, eds. Robert L. Zahn and Meyer N. Zald (San Francisco: Jossey-Bass, 1990).

25. Bazerman, *Judgment in Managerial Decision Making*, 62

26. This is in contrast to "bounded rationality," which we discussed in an earlier chapter.

27. Richard Thaler, "From Homo Economicus to Homo Sapiens," *Journal of Economic Perspectives* 14, no. 1 (2000).

28. Samuel M. McClure, David I. Laibson, George Loewenstein, and Jonathan D. Cohen, "Separate Neural Systems Value Immediate and Delayed Monetary Rewards," *Science* 306 (2004), 503–507.

29. Adam Smith, *The Wealth of Nations* (New York: Prometheus Books, 1991).

30. Paul R. Lawrence and Nitin Nohria, *Driven: How Human Nature Shapes Our Choices* (San Francisco: Jossey-Bass, 2002).

31. The alert reader will note that we do not start off with a list of the uncertainties in the decision, as we did with misleading experiences and prejudgments. This is because self-interest can operate even when there is no, or limited, uncertainty. For example, there was little uncertainty at Enron that cashing out one's own options at a high price, while hiding the true state of the company from the public and the markets, was not a good decision from the perspective of most of the stakeholders involved. But it did not stop managers deciding to do this. Of course, self-interest may have a more powerful effect where uncertainty is highest—the greater the uncertainty, the more likely it is that the decision makers can persuade themselves that they are making an objective decision when they are not. However, it would overly constrain our search for red flags to limit it to where there is uncertainty. Hence, we take the rather more intuitive route of thinking about each option in turn and considering whether the decision maker's interests might be affected were that option chosen.

Chapter 8

1. Reuters, "Wolfowitz Nominated for World Bank Post," Dow Jones Factiva, March 16, 2005, http://factiva.com/.

2. World Bank, "Biography of Paul Wolfowitz," http://go.worldbank.org/73A9LU5D60>.

3. World Bank, "Second Report of the Ad Hoc Group," 10–11, May 14, 2007, http://go.worldbank.org/HQ1DWS0VI0.

4. World Bank, "Ethics Committee and Procedures," 1, October 20, 2003, http://go.worldbank.org/U85V0MAS60.

5. World Bank, "Second Report of the Ad Hoc Group," 13.

6. Ibid., 14.

7. World Bank, "Personnel Package," 5–8, April 14, 2007, http://go.worldbank.org/SN6P8R8XK0.

8. World Bank, "Second Report of the Ad Hoc Group," 15–16.

9. Ibid., 18.

10. Ibid., 31–33.

11. That Wolfowitz seemed unconcerned about leaving a paper trail suggests that he, for one, did not believe he was doing anything wrong. As is the case for other emotional red flags, the decision maker, when left to his own devices, is often the last person to know that his decisions are flawed.

12. World Bank, "Second Report of the Ad Hoc Group," 19–21.

13. Ibid., 35–36.

14. Ibid., 24.

15. The EC is not without fault either. Despite having emphasized the preliminary nature of its earlier recommendation to Wolfowitz, the EC did not question him and did not ask for the details of the agreement. The EC considered the issue closed and informed the board of executive directors that the situation was resolved. The board agreed. What's more, EC chairman Melkert later sent a handwritten note to Wolfowitz thanking him for his "open and constructive spirit" in discussions regarding this "extraordinarily difficult issue." Melkert also noted that this issue was particularly sensitive for "Shaha" (Riza). He went on to invite Wolfowitz and Riza to join him for a social gathering at his place. However, the EC's failings do not excuse Wolfowitz's.

16. World Bank, "Second Report of the Ad Hoc Group," 25.

17. Ibid., 26.

18. Al Kamen, "Where the Money Is," *Washington Post*, March 28, 2007, online at Dow Jones Factiva, http://factiva.com/.

19. World Bank, "Statement—Executive Directors Review Report, Release Documents," April 12, 2007, http://go.worldbank.org/38T3UYNND0.

20. World Bank, "Second Report of the Ad Hoc Group," 17.

21. Ibid., 43–44.

22. World Bank, "Statement by Paul Wolfowitz," April 12, 2007, http://go.worldbank .org/1XKL327XC0.

23. World Bank, "Statements of the Executive Directors and President Wolfowitz," May 17, 2007, http://go.worldbank.org/NDB91EQRJ0.

24. Adam Smith, *The Theory of Moral Sentiments* (London: Millar, Kincaid and Bell, 1759), 47.

25. Charles Darwin, *The Descent of Man* (Amherst, NY: Prometheus Books, 1998), 111.

26. Paul R. Lawrence and Nitin Nohria, *Driven: How Human Nature Shapes Our Choices* (San Francisco: Jossey-Bass, 2002).

27. Robert Trivers, "The Evolution of Reciprocal Altruism," *Quarterly Review of Biology* 46 (1992).

28. More precisely, these characteristics evolved because the genes of women who valued them had a higher chance of being reproduced in future generations.

29. Geoffrey Miller, *The Mating Mind: How Sexual Choice Shaped the Evolution of Human Nature* (London: Heinemann, 2000), 306–340.

30. David M. Buss et al., "International Preferences in Selecting Mates: A Study of 37 Cultures," *Journal of Cross-Cultural Psychology* 21 (1990).

31. George Loewenstein, Leigh Thompson, and Max H. Bazerman, "Social Utility and Decision Making in Interpersonal Contexts," *Journal of Personality and Social Psychology* 57, no. 3 (1989). Note that we have simplified the description of the structure of study to make it more digestible for the reader. We refer particularly to study 2 of the three studies covered in the paper.

32. Mid-level manager at Samsung, interview by author, May 17, 2000.

33. Roger Dean Du Mars, "Tough Act to Follow," Asiaweek.com. November 16, 2001, http://www.ircltd.com/media/2001NovemberAsiaWeekToughActToFollow.pdf.

34. Sydney Finkelstein, *Why Smart Executives Fail and What You Can Learn from Their Mistakes* (New York: Portfolio, 2003), 34.

35. Ibid, 32.

36. Craig Conway, "PeopleSoft—from Turnaround to Target" lecture at Said Business School, University of Oxford, UK, September 22, 2005), http://www.sbs.ox.ac.uk/news/ archives/Events/From+turnaround+to+target.htm.

37. Scott Ard, "Notable Quotes: Hostile Bid Ignites the Rhetoric," *CNET News.com*, December 13, 2004, http://www.news.com/2100-1014_3-5489353.html.

38. Like the instinct to bond, the skill of making a distinction between us and them seems to also be built in. It is known as the *dyadic instinct* and is the basis for identifying

the group to which one is attached, but also the outsiders to whom one feels hostile; see Lawrence and Nohria, *Driven*, 102.

39. David Brown, "Boy, 14, Is Latest Victim of Gang Violence," *Times Online*, April 9, 2007, http://www.timesonline.co.uk/tol/news/uk/crime/article1629551.ece.

40. For further discussion, see Jonathan Barron, *Thinking and Deciding*, 3rd ed. (Cambridge: Cambridge University Press, 2000), 454.

41. Ibid., 445–447.

42. Judi Bevan, *The Rise and Fall of Marks & Spencer . . . And How It Rose Again*, 2nd ed. (London: Profile Books, 2007), 81.

43. Judi Bevan, interview by author, March 2008.

44. Bevan, *The Rise and Fall of Marks & Spencer*, 84.

45. Ibid., 72.

Chapter 9

1. Alexander Fursenko and Timothy J. Naftali, *One Hell of a Gamble* (London: John Murray 1997), 88.

2. Elie Abel, *The Missile Crisis* (New York: Bantam, 1966).

3. Graham T. Allison, *Essence of Decision: Explaining the Cuban Missile Crisis* (Boston: Little, Brown, 1971), 57.

4. Roger Hilsman, *To Move a Nation: The Politics of Foreign Policy in the Adminis-tration of John F. Kennedy* (Garden City, NY: Doubleday, 1967).

5. Elizabeth Corcoran, "The E Gang," *Forbes*, http://www.forbes.com/forbes/2000/0724/6603145a.html.

6. Paul Rogers and Marcia Blenko, "Who Has the D? How Clear Decision Roles En-hance Organizational Performance," *Harvard Business Review*, January 2006.

7. Michael A. Roberto, *Why Great Leaders Don't Take Yes for an Answer: Managing for Conflict and Consensus* (Upper Saddle River, NJ: Wharton School Publishing, 2005), 52.

8. We do not discuss here potentially alternative ways to split the roles—for example, creating a role that is similar to that of chairman but with a different title, such as lead di-rector. For a discussion, see Paul Coombes and Simon Chiu-Yin Wong, "Chairman and CEO—One Job or Two?" *McKinsey Quarterly*, no. 2 (2004).

9. Jill Treanor and Julia Finch, "Shareholder Unease at Elevation of Chairman Rose," *Guardian* (Manchester), March 11, 2008.

10. Karen Attwood, "Investors Attack M&S Plan to Make Rose Chairman," *Independent* (London), March 11, 2008.

11. Shareholders accounting for more than 20 percent of the retailer's institutional base voiced their opposition to the move, according to a poll carried out by the *Sunday Times*. Dissenters included more than ten of Britain's most powerful pension funds. The findings challenged M&S's assertion that it had broad support for its reshuffle, which defies board-room best-practice codes. James Ashton and Jenny Davey, "Storm Grows over Stuart Rose's Chairman Role at Marks & Spencer," *Sunday Times* (London), 2008, http://business.timesonline.co.uk/tol/business/industry_sectors/retailing/article3638573.ece.

12. Lisa Buckingham and Neil Craven, "Search Is on for Top Non-Execs at M&S," *Fi-nancial Mail* (London), 2008, http://www.thisismoney.co.uk/investing-and-markets/article.html?in_article_id=437954&in_page_id=3.

13. Robert F. Felton, "Splitting Chairs: Should CEOs Give Up the Chairman's Role? An Interview with Jack Creighton," *McKinsey Quarterly*, no. 4 (2004).

14. John Mayo, "Exploding Some Marconi Myths," *Financial Times* (London), January 18, 2002.

15. This was reported in a BBC program, *The Blair Years*, in November 2007, by Hans Blix, the head of the Iraq inspection team. Blix explained that Chirac had confided in him personally that he did not believe there were any weapons of mass destruction in Iraq. Blix challenged him, saying that Chirac's own intelligence agency was claiming information

about such weapons. Chirac's reply was somewhat dismissive of his intelligence agency, claiming that it frequently became overenthusiastic about such threats.

16. Ex-Israeli intelligence officer, interview by author.

17. Katherine L. Milkman, Dolly Chugh, and Max H. Bazerman. "How Can Decision Making Be Improved?" Harvard Business School, Working paper, 2008, 3.

18. Ibid, 2.

Chapter 10

1. Steve Russell, interview by author.

Chapter 11

1. Roger Crockett, "How Motorola Lost Its Way," *Business Week*, May 4, 1998, 140.

INDEX

ABOUT THE AUTHORS

Sydney Finkelstein is the Steven Roth Professor of Management at Dartmouth's Tuck School of Business and Director of the Tuck Executive Program. He is widely known as one of the world's leading authorities on strategy and leadership, and has served as a consultant for companies around the globe. He is a Fellow of the Academy of Management and the author of more than ten books, including the international bestseller, *Why Smart Executives Fail*.

Jo Whitehead is a director of the Ashridge Strategic Management Centre. An engineering graduate from Cambridge University, he has an MBA from Harvard Business School and a PhD in business strategy and organizational behavior from London Business School. He has extensive global experience as a consultant working with The Boston Consulting Group in the United States and in Europe.

Andrew Campbell has been a director of the London-based Ashridge Strategic Management Centre, part of Ashridge Business School, since 1987. Previously, he was on the faculty of London Business School and a consultant at McKinsey & Company. He is an expert on business strategy and author of more than ten books, including the classic text *Corporate-Level Strategy*, and six articles in the *Harvard Business Review*, including the popular "What Is Wrong with Strategy?"